EDITORIAL

Avoiding a state of solitude

Worrying about a local newspaper closing or reporters being centralised is not just nostalgia, it's being concerned that our democratic watchdogs are going missing, says **Rachael Jolley**

48(01): 01/03 I DOI: 10.1177/0306422019842456

REGIONAL UK DAILY newspaper the Eastern Daily Press is closing two of its district offices, in Cromer on the north Norfolk coast, and in Diss, a Norfolk market town.

This matters to me because the EDP was the first place I worked as a journalist and it was then one of the UK's biggest local papers, with at least 10 offices, all employing reporters. Some of the offices had one or two reporters, some had 10, and the Norwich head office had about 50 editorial staff.

When I joined as a trainee reporter, the big bosses mandated that we worked in at least three different offices within two years. We went out and about on an almost daily basis, talking to people and covering events.

These days, national newspaper editors dream of having as many reporters as the EDP had in the 1990s.

So why does this matter? And should anyone care when the small newspaper office in Cromer closes? After all, as the management of the EDP said, everyone is online now, so we can do business digitally. And, yes, most of us can communicate by email (although not everyone, as our story on p46 shows) and we could email our news tips to a far-flung newsdesk.

We could, but perhaps we won't bother.

And, yes, you can do business digitally: we can send money and adverts around the world at the click of a mouse. But the stuff at the guts of a local newspaper, the finding out what is going on and hearing a sniff of a story in the pub, will that still go on or will reporters be left to depend on social media as a source?

If no local reporters are left living and working in these communities, are they really going to care about those places? Will they even know who to call, or who to email? When a massive fire starts down by the King's Lynn docks, will anyone from the local newspaper be there to see it (as I was one midnight when I saw the flames out of my bedroom window)?

The answer is clearly that they will not. News will go unreported; stories will not be told; people will not know what has happened in their towns and communities.

Local newspapers (and, to some extent, local radio stations) were, and in some places still are, fighting for the little guy against the monolith for the old person, say, who is inundated by noisy construction work morning, noon and night. They bring to the attention of the →

EDITOR
Rachael Jolley

DEPUTY EDITOR
Sally Gimson

SUB EDITORS
Tracey Bagshaw,
Adam Aiken

CONTRIBUTING EDITORS
Irene Caselli (Argentina),
Jan Fox (USA),
Kaya Genç (Turkey),
Laura Silvia Battaglia
(Yemen and Iraq),
Stephen Woodman
(Mexico)

EDITORIAL ASSISTANT
Lewis Jennings

ART DIRECTOR
Matthew Hasteley

COVER
Ben Jennings

THANKS TO
Sebastian Borger,
Sean Gallagher,
Ryan McChrystal

MAGAZINE PRINTED BY
Page Bros.,
Norwich UK

INDEX ON CENSORSHIP
indexoncensorship.org I +44 (0) 20 3848 9820 I 1 Rivington Place, London EC2A 3BA, United Kingdom

Supported by
ARTS COUNCIL ENGLAND

→ public a council plan to close a massively popular library, or a bid to cement over a local swimming pool and turn it into flats. They cover a big crown court case about a million-pound corruption that ends with shops closing and jobs being lost.

When things went wrong, the local media were there to make sure people knew about it, and what the problems were. They could knock on the door of the powerful and shout for something to change.

And, yes, these things don't have to be done only in print – a website can still cover stories and reach an audience – but if there are no re-porters on the ground, and they are increasingly based far away from the stories they cover, they will increasingly miss knowing about scandals, corruption and the death of the totally brilliant grandmother who was the heart of the place.

One ex-newspaperman told me he recently walked into a city office to find all the staff for local newspapers from one part of Scotland sitting there, together. They had all become long-distance reporters, at arm's length from the places they reported on.

This is more than an industrial tip-ping point. This is a gradual unpicking of part of democ-racy: scandals that need to be held up to the light will get missed; local au-thorities that spend public money will have no one watch-ing to see if they are doing it according to the rules.

There is also cause to worry about the coverage of the courts and the justice system. As the former lord chief justice of England and Wales, Lord Judge, told

Index: "Open justice is one of the essential safeguards of the rule of law. The presence of the media in our courts represents the public's entitlement to witness the administration of justice and assess whether, and how, justice is being done. As the number of newspapers declines and fewer journalists attend court, particularly in courts outside London and the major cities, and except in high-profile cases, the necessary public scrutiny of the judicial process will be steadily eroded, eventually to virtual extinction."

Lord Judge is right. It is likely that budget-stretched local newspaper managers will drop the coverage that costs them the most money. The difficult stuff will get ignored and replaced with fun videos of cats and other animals. The person who sifts steadily through a council agenda, page by page, will disappear, to be replaced by a "content manager" whose job is to produce crowd-pleasing clickbait fare.

Mike Sassi, editor of the Nottingham Post in the UK, said: "There's no doubt that local decision-makers aren't subject to the level of scrutiny they once were. There are large numbers of councils right across the country making big decisions, involving millions of pounds of public money, who may never see a local reporter. Many local authorities will be operating in the knowl-edge that no one will ever ask them an awkward question. Which, obviously enough, does nothing to help build trust in local democracy."

The problem, some argue, is that the public are not really bothered about losing these skills or services. If they were, they would be willing to support them. Local news has to be paid for, and the companies that have been producing it have to make money to survive. If the public don't care enough to pay for it, they will move on to doing other things. That's the way the market works.

People are willing to pay for a cinema ticket, or to go to the football, or for a Netflix subscrip-tion, but right now it appears that not many are willing to pay for local news. And if no one funds it, it disappears. Will it be a case of appreciating local news reporting only when it is gone?

There's even more to worry about when it comes to news vacuums appearing. As people

feel more and more disconnected from the place where they live, they move into a state of solitude, not knowing what is going on around them. That breeds discontent, a feeling of being ignored, and when a community doesn't exist there's no one to lean on when things go wrong.

There is a public right to information about what locally elected officials are doing, but there is no public right to a newspaper. If no one wants to buy it, and if no one cares about it, it is likely to disappear. But there is a lot more to lose than a place when you find detailed coverage of your local football team (much appreciated though that is by many). There are deep societal costs.

There are some signs of public discontent which may be linked to declining local news coverage, and might be a sign that people are waking up to what is going missing when local media operations close down or pull away from certain types of coverage.

For this issue, we commissioned YouGov to carry out a poll of the public and we found that 40% of British adults over the age of 65 think that the public know less about what is happening in areas where local newspapers have closed down.

Also, Libby Purves, a columnist at The Times who started her career on a local radio station, tells us she believes part of the discontent that produced Brexit was about people in far-flung places and regional cities feeling their news and views were being ignored (see p40). She also talks to us about her earlier years working on Radio Oxford and the close relationship the station had with people who worked in and around the city. They would march into the centrally located studio and tell reporters when they were getting it wrong, she says.

The question is: how can that be replaced today? Can it be done on social media, for instance? Or is it a bit like barking at a tree? You have made noise, but the tree definitely isn't listening?

For those of you who thought that threats to local news were just in your own country, think again. We looked into this issue around the globe and found some of the same problems developing in China, Argentina, the USA and

Proper journalism cannot be replaced by people tweeting their opinions and the occasional photo of a squirrel, no matter how amusing the squirrel might be

Belgium, among others. We interviewed people in Italy, Germany, India, the UK and Nigeria. The worries are often the same, the reasons slightly different.

Many of those who fight for freedom of expression feel that declining numbers of local reporters just make it easier for governments to cover up scandals, leave the public ill-informed, and make sure only the information they want is out there.

There are some bright sparks who have ideas about how the important services that local news has provided could work differently in the future. There are people starting their own local paper, focusing on digging out stories, growing circulation and making enough money to keep going (see p20).

Other ideas are also emerging. The BBC's local democracy reporters project, discussed in this magazine, is one way of funding specialists who have time to dig through council agendas to find out what is going on. What about finding specialist bloggers with in-depth knowledge on their particular local magistrates' court, for instance, and having a Gofundme campaign to get up to 3,000 locals to pay £5 or £10 a month for a twice-weekly email of fabulously detailed and incisive analysis of what is happening?

Big ideas are needed. Democracy loses if local news disappears. Sadly, those long-held checks and balances are fracturing, and there are few replacements on the horizon. Proper journalism cannot be replaced by people tweeting their opinions and the occasional photo of a squirrel, no matter how amusing the squirrel might be. ⊗

Rachael Jolley Editor, Index on Censorship

CONTENTS

VOLUME 48 NUMBER 01 – SPRING 2019

CREDIT: Ben Jennings

IN FOCUS

CULTURE

SPECIAL REPORT

The future is robotic

Computers are now being used to generate local news stories. **Mark Frary** asks if it will leave reporters free to dig deeper

48(01): 08/10 I DOI: 10.1177/0306422019842082

IF YOU READ a newspaper this week, there is a chance that some of the stories were written not by a flesh and blood journalist but by a machine.

Publishers are increasingly using "robot reporters" to generate the simpler stories that used to be written by junior hacks, but can now be created by simply plugging data into a standard story template.

The argument goes that if journalists can be freed up from writing cookie-cutter stories, they can spend their time more fruitfully, holding the powerful to account.

The cynics argue that publishers, increasingly run by accountants rather than creative types, are simply trying to cut costs.

Bloomberg News editor-in-chief John Micklethwait says a quarter of the content produced by the news giant has some degree of automation.

It uses a system called Cyborg which "dissects a company's earnings the moment they appear and produces not just instant headlines but, in a matter of seconds, what is in effect a mini-wrap with all the numbers and a lot of context".

And it is not the only one using robot reporters. The Washington Post has developed a bot called Heliograf that automatically generates stories from sports results.

Meredith Broussard, an assistant professor at the Arthur L Carter Journalism Institute of New York University, says that while earnings reports are ripe for automation, other types of news story are not.

The potential of artificial intelligence to write more than just templated news stories is already with us. An Elon Musk-funded initiative called OpenAI has developed an AI-powered text engine known as GPT-2. Trained on millions of pages of text from the web, the engine predicts the next word in a piece of text and can write "deep fake" news stories. The stories, to the untrained eye, are virtually indistinguishable from those written by real journalists. The company has said it is so concerned about the potential for misuse of the technology that it is holding back from releasing the research in order to understand its implications more fully.

Broussard, a computer scientist turned data journalist, sits at the crossroads of AI and news reporting. Her team developed a tool called Bailiwick, which helped visualise campaign finance data related to the 2016 US election.

She says a high-profile investigative story might take years to put together and require lots of document analysis: the cost of which can stretch into the millions.

"My projects are inexpensive in comparison. That is important for innovation," she said.

But Broussard does not believe that AI will replace journalists.

"There is this idea that technology is always the best solution – I call it technochauvinism," she said. "There has been this idea that we can use fewer reporters and they can learn everything from social media. That has proven to be untrue."

Many see the role of AI as a tool to help journalists rather than replace them. For those in local journalism, where newspapers are dying at an unprecedented rate, it may represent a way to avoid extinction.

Toby Abel, chief technology officer of Krzana, a company arming local news publishers with AI tools, said: "The advertising model [has been] useless for local journalism ever since social media came to the fore. We are seeing the opportunity of new funding models with the emphasis much more on the value and trust of the reader. Instead of an advertiser paying, the reader pays.

"The role of AI is to take the bits of journalism that are essentially busy work and try to replace those with cheap and quick solutions that get out of journalists' way."

Krzana – a pun in Sanskrit that means both the act of finding pearls and a human pulse – is a tool which says it is "trying to let people keep [a] finger on what is going on and finding nuggets of information".

It draws together tens of thousands of real-time content feeds – social media, police blogs, local government minutes – and crunches them with AI tools, most of them proprietary.

"Journalists tell us they want to know whenever someone talks about a certain type of crime in Birmingham, for example," said Abel.

He is dismissive of initiatives that aim to replace human journalists with robot reporters, saying: "The consequence has been horrible, watered-down, clickbaity journalism where they have tried."

And it is not just large newspaper groups that are using Krzana.

The West Bridgford Wire is a hyperlocal news website, based in Nottingham, that gets up to a million page views every month.

Abel said: "It has quadrupled readership in the last 12 months through being able to source stories with just one guy doing deep investigative journalism. That seems like the future."

Many publishers use content aggregation tools such as Tweetdeck, but The Wire's editor, Pat Gamble, says Krzana is smarter. "It has a magical way of cleaning things up. Most things that come up are useful."

Gamble uses Krzana on a daily basis and says a major benefit is that stories come up as they are published, rather than just when they are tweeted, allowing him to get a headstart.

And he says the site is constantly picking up new advertisers who like the fresh and relevant content it publishes.

Some of the funding for the increased use of AI in local and regional journalism is coming from two of the companies that have done much to take advertising away from local →

It has quadrupled readership in the last 12 months through being able to source stories with just one guy doing deep investigative journalism

There is this idea that technology is always the best solution – I call it technochauvinism

→ news publishers, even though they thrive on their output – Facebook and Google.

In January 2017, the Facebook Journalism Project was introduced "to establish stronger ties between Facebook and the news industry". Its goals were to develop collaborative news products and provide training and tools for both journalists and individuals.

It has since held several hackathons (events where developers gather to create software products) attended by news organisations, some of which have seen teams develop AI tools.

Google's News Initiative was launched the following year and aims to "empower news organisations through technological innovation".

Abel, of Krzana, said: "I think here is a danger [the funding] gets used as a crutch to allow local journalism to continue not to make money. It should be used as a stepping stone. An injection of capital is a great way to solve a bootstrapping problem to move towards sustainable local journalism."

One project that has received funding from Google is an AI-powered tool called Inject, which was built by a team led by Neil Maiden, professor of digital creativity at London's Cass Business School.

Like a search engine, Inject builds an index from hundreds of sources every day and this now contains more than 10 million news stories.

"We have written a number of algorithms – you might call it creative search. Google gives you exactly what you ask for. If you put something in our tool, it takes what you write and looks for something similar but different," said Maiden.

Inject focuses on finding an angle for a journalist to cover, whether that is data, the human angle, the long read or something quirky or funny.

To create the algorithms that drive Inject, Maiden's team worked with experienced local journalists and politicians to rate news stories on various criteria and use the data to work out what makes a "good" story.

"We are not making the journalists more creative; we are trying to make them as creative as they would be, but faster," he said.

Vincent Peyregne, CEO of the World Association of Newspapers and News Publishers, feels that AI offers a lifeline to some, and a new way of working for others.

"In Africa, there is strong interest in AI due to the limited resources they have. AI is an opportunity to improve and grow," he said.

He believes the biggest challenge for wider adoption of AI is not the technology, saying: "It is about changing the workflow and culture of your organisation. The bottleneck is in management." ⊗

WHO IS USING AI FOR NEWS GATHERING?

The Washington Post: uses Heliograf to collect data for articles about election races too numerous to cover individually, and sporting events. Journalists add analysis and colour

Rheinische Post: a regional German newspaper, uses its Listening Center to collate information about what people in their region are talking about on the internet so they can use it to create stories

PA: uses Reporters and Data and Robots to create multiple, localised versions of stories sourced from open data sets from central government, local authorities and other public services, to sell to local newspapers

The Express Tribune: in Pakistan used Krzana technology during the general election, monitoring events from general gossip to political murders

Hallingdølen: is one of several local newspapers in Norway that trialled the use of Inject technology to help create news stories

Sally Gimson

Mark Frary is a journalist and author. He wrote De/Cipher, a guide to cryptography, and is working on an account of the rise of technology company Psion

Terrorising the truth

Local Mexican journalists on the US border are so intimidated by drug cartels they are afraid to report the news, writes **Stephen Woodman**

48(01): 11/13 | DOI: 10.1177/0306422019842083

THIS YEAR, MEXICO will once again mark World Press Freedom Day on 3 May with a surge in column inches devoted to freedom of expression issues. But no one expects any let-up in the media crisis engulfing Tamaulipas, the country's infamous "silent zone".

In this border state facing Texas, newspapers keep quiet on the region's rampant cartel activity. Instead, locals turn to anonymous Twitter accounts for updates on shootouts and blockades.

With crimes against the press threatening local media across the country, Tamaulipas offers a nightmare vision of what could lie ahead, a violent state where violence and self-censorship have left citizens in the dark.

In December last year, a box containing the severed head and hands of an unidentified man was left outside the offices of the Expreso newspaper in Ciudad Victoria, the state capital. "The fear is a constant," an Expreso journalist told Index, on condition he remained anonymous.

A box containing the severed head and hands of an unidentified man was left outside the offices of the Expreso newspaper in Ciudad Victoria

"The criminals know who you are, where you live and how many family members you have. They know everything."

The media blackout began its slow descent in February 2000 with the murder of Luis Roberto Cruz, a reporter for Multicosas magazine in the border city of Reynosa. Thirteen more journalists have been killed in Tamaulipas since, according to press freedom watchdog Article 19.

The violence intensified in 2006 when assailants opened fire on the offices of El Mañana newspaper, in the city of Nuevo Laredo, detonating a grenade and paralysing a journalist. The Inter-American Commission on Human Rights described the event as "the first attack using weapons and explosives against the facilities of a media outlet during the war on drug trafficking".

The media silence in Tamaulipas is tied to the state's strategic location in Mexico's ongoing drug war. Cartels have long smuggled cocaine and other contraband through Altamira port on the Gulf Coast. The 17 border crossings with Texas also provide access to the illegal drugs market in the USA.

Turf wars between competing criminal factions have raged ever since Los Zetas, a paramilitary group linked to the Gulf cartel, broke ties with their former allies almost 10 years ago, and the local press has increasingly become a pawn in the hands of cartel commanders.

Criminals force media workers to limit reports of violence in order that their illegal activities can continue uninterrupted, and without the government deploying extra troops or police. But cartels occasionally commit deliberate acts of violence in order to force a government crackdown, a practice known as "heating up" a rival's turf. In such instances, cartel operatives will demand newspapers send reporters to cover the story. Compromised journalists, known as *enlaces*, or links, manage this practice of editorial encroachment. The *enlaces* work for the cartels and make sure newspapers publish certain stories and censor others.

This elaborate system grew in response to the intensity of the cartel conflict in Tamaulipas, says Guadalupe Correa author of the

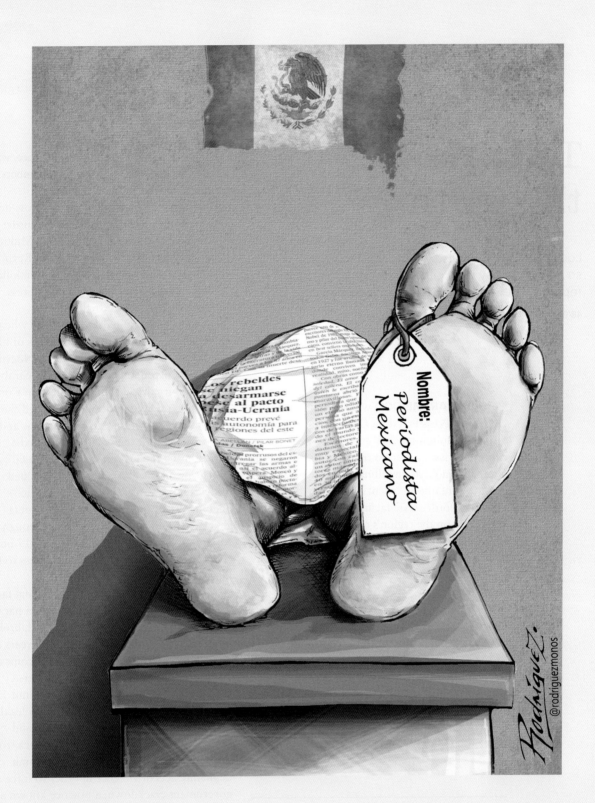

→ book Los Zetas Inc: Criminal Corporations, Energy, and Civil War in Mexico.

"You have groups that are highly militarised and you have the government going after them," she said. "That generates incentives to control information as if it were a war between armies."

The restrictions on the press mean many rely on citizen reporters such as Loba Indomable (Indomitable Wolf). Loba uses Twitter to provide drug war news, uploading graphic photographs of crime scenes or videos of gunfights provided by concerned citizens. She tweets the updates she believes to be authentic and tries to sift out empty rumours or cartel propaganda. Loba told Index she was motivated by a desire to keep law-abiding citizens safe. However,

Loba uses Twitter to provide drug war news, uploading graphic photographs of crime scenes or videos of gunfights provided by concerned citizens

she accepts there are significant downsides to citizen journalism.

"Not all of the social media accounts are trustworthy," she said. "There are accounts falsely claiming to be linked to the army. I know they are fake, but others might be taken in."

In recent years, cartels have increasingly targeted online reporters, including Loba.

But cartel bosses are not the only people threatening press freedom in Tamaulipas. Politicians are also linked to silencing critical voices. In January last year, masked assailants stabbed political columnist Carlos Domínguez Rodríguez to death in his car when he stopped at traffic lights in Nuevo Laredo. The late reporter's son, also called Carlos Domínguez, believes the former mayor of Nuevo Laredo was behind the killing. Six suspects were arrested in connection to the crime, including three journalists and the former mayor's nephew.

Domínguez told Index that writing about politicians was more dangerous for journalists than reporting on drug traffickers, especially as the line between the two had become increasingly blurred in recent years.

"If they keep targeting reporters, we will end up without any information that is uncomfortable for the government," Domínguez said. "We cannot say we live in a democracy when freedom of expression is not guaranteed." ⊗

Stephen Woodman *is contributing editor, Mexico, for Index on Censorship. He is based in Guadalajara*

DYING FOR LOCAL NEWS

Regional journalists frequently write not only stories, but their own death warrants.

TAMAULIPAS IS NOT the only Mexican state where cartels and politicians target local media.

According to Article 19, 122 journalists have been killed across the country in connection with their work since 2000. Three in every four of these murders occurred in the northern frontier or southern states.

Blighted by drug cartels drawn to their border crossings and seaports, these regions also suffer from widespread political corruption.

Local journalists are at particular risk in this environment, with 95% of those killed for their work reporting for local outlets, according to the Committee to Protect Journalists. Given that trend, there is a real danger of more "silent zones" emerging in Mexico.

The border state of Chihuahua came under the international spotlight in 2017 when its largest daily newspaper, Norte de Ciudad Juarez, closed due to security concerns. The publication returned with 15 special editions last year but has not resumed daily circulation.

In recent years, violence against the press has risen most sharply in Mexico's poor southern zone. In Guerrero state, criminals have increasingly sought to control local media as the region becomes the main supplier of heroin to the USA.

But nowhere has deteriorated more than the south-eastern state of Veracruz, which became Mexico's deadliest place for journalists in 2012.

Just below Tamaulipas on the map, the state shares the cartel problem ravaging the Gulf Coast. But many reporters in Veracruz still cover shootouts and massacres, in contrast to colleagues in Tamaulipas.

"A small sector of the press held firm in its decision to report on these incidents," said the Inter-American Commission on Human Rights in a 2017 report.

The refusal to censor has come at a great cost. Seventeen reporters were killed during the 2010-16 term of former state governor Javier Duarte, who is now serving a nine-year prison sentence for corruption.

"Writing a story might mean signing your own death sentence during the Duarte era, says Santos Solis, the director-general of the digital newspaper Oye Veracruz.

Solis says the "journalism of fear" that Duarte fostered has persisted despite his removal from office. "If the government does not act, we will end up like Tamaulipas," he predicted.

Switched off

The media has been a political football in Argentina for years. Now, as **Irene Caselli** reports, people are losing confidence in local news and are looking for alternatives

48(01): 14/17 I DOI: 10.1177/0306422019842084

ARGENTINA'S ELECTION MACHINE is revving up ahead of the presidential election in October. But as journalists and media owners struggle, people are looking to other, less traditional outlets for their news.

And that is worrying commentators who blame the election in Brazil of the far-right populist president Jair Bolsonaro, in part on the influence of unreliable Whatsapp groups and "fake news" sites. They wonder whether there could be a similar rise in populism in Argentina where people are losing confidence in the established local media.

The crisis in journalism is acute. Newspapers and news agencies are closing, journalists are losing their jobs and people say they do not trust traditional news outlets any more.

Since Mauricio Macri took over as president of Argentina three years ago, more than 3,000 journalists have lost their jobs, according to the Forum of Argentine Journalism (Fopea).

El Gráfico, one of Latin America's most prestigious sport magazines, closed down in 2018 after 99 years on the market; the English-language daily Buenos Aires Herald disappeared after 140 years; and regional media laid off workers and contributors including at Río Negro, Patagonia's largest newspaper.

The private national news agency Diaros y Noticias (Dyn) closed in November 2017, and in June 2018 the state-run agency Telam laid off journalists and its overall output went down.

"Dyn was the only strong and independent agency in Argentina," said Daniel Dessein, president of La Gaceta, the largest newspaper in north-western Argentina. "It reported on what happened in every province beyond Buenos Aires. Now, in terms of information, provinces have fewer channels to learn about what happens in the rest of the country. It is generating an insularity effect."

Martín Becerra, Argentina's leading media analyst, told Index that there were "broad consequences for freedom of expression" after these closures. "Society as a whole is affected by the decline of sources for local and regional information as well as professionally edited perspectives," he said.

Dessein agrees: "Democracy is undoubtedly affected by the decline in the journalistic flow, quality and rigour and by the decline of diversity and plurality of voices. All this affects public debate."

In response to this crisis other outlets are setting up shop. Chani Guyot worked for 20 years as an editor at La Nación, one of Argentina's largest newspapers. In 2017, he left his role as editor-in-chief and started Redacción, a digital enterprise dedicated to local stories.

Guyot views Redacción as an antidote to the media crisis: "We claim we are doing human journalism," he said. The publication, which finances itself thanks to private donations and a membership model, focuses on social issues that are not covered by other media.

Redacción is part of a new landscape of digital media that create alternative coverage. Chequeado, Cosecha Roja, Revista Anfibia,

Society as a whole is affected by the decline of sources for local and regional information as well as professionally edited perspectives

Latfem, lavaca and Futurock radio, which are funded by members or thanks to grants, are among the most prestigious.

For Hinde Pomeraniec, culture editor at the Infobae news portal, it is social networks, which are providing the diversity of opinions and information that the media now lack.

"When I get asked what to read in order to get a balanced opinion, what I recommend is to follow specific journalists more than media," she told Index. "Because you may find very rigorous journalists working for media that you do not trust."

Néstor Sclauzero, news manager of the state-run TV Pública, and president of Fopea, also believes that the digital world is creating new opportunities. In television, for example, costs have become much lower, giving regional media new opportunities.

"Before, it was impossible to set up a TV station. Now with a smartphone and a laptop you can produce a decent TV report and make it circulate," he said.

The crisis which has struck Argentina's traditional media is not unlike what is happening worldwide, where the painful transition into the digital age has led to layoffs. What makes the crisis of Argentina's media more acute is that it went through a brief period of bonanza just as the rest of the world started readjusting some 10 years ago.

Under the previous presidency of Cristina Fernández de Kirchner, the government poured millions into advertising that partly financed the creation of new media aligned to the government. It was part of Fernández de Kirchner's battle against private media concentration.

For example, over the 2009-2015 period, pro-government Grupo Veintitrés was the largest receiver of advertising funds, receiving $53 million, according to La Nación newspaper.

That money partly financed the opening of new media, such as the newspaper Tiempo Argentino. The connection to Fernández de Kirchner was apparent in the paper's editorial position, which was supportive of the government's social-oriented policies and vocal against the opposition – so much so that critics accused it of publishing propaganda.

When Macri took over, Grupo Veintitrés saw its close relationship with the government end abruptly. The owners disappeared, leaving journalists stranded without pay. At Tiempo Argentino, staff got together and started functioning as a co-operative, which is still going strong after three years.

"Advertising was supposed to be an incentive, but it had two limitations: it concentrated on traditional media at a time when digital media were gaining ground, and it did not actually improve the quality of journalism," said Adriana Amado, president of Infociudadana, an NGO dedicated to improving the quality of information for citizens. "It was like steroids. When the money came to an end, the muscles did not last."

The crisis hit all media, regardless of ideology, because all benefited from government advertising. However, given Argentina's concentrated media market was in the capital, Buenos Aires, those who took the hardest hit were smaller, regional media.

Things became even harder in 2018, when the economy shrank by 2.8% and inflation hit a 27-year high of 47.6%. →

ELSEWHERE IN LATIN AMERICA...

Social networks and online media are the new ways journalists have found to produce independent news and circumvent government control

IN VENEZUELA, WHERE the government of Nicolás Maduro has kept news coverage under control over the past years and reporters have been arrested and harassed for their coverage, digital media such as ArmandoInfo or Efecto Cocuyo have become a source of independent information both inside and outside the country.

In Paraguay, where there are no legal limits on media concentration, El Surtidor was born in 2016 as an antidote to the mainstream narrative. It is a visual journalism platform where features are often presented as comics. It is led by a not-for-profit co-operative of journalists and mainly sustained by grants and a membership model.

In Brazil, the membership model has made it possible for media such as Agência Pública to carry out investigations into environmental or social issues that are not usually tackled by established media.

When I get asked what to read in order to get a balanced opinion, what I recommend is to follow specific journalists more than media

→ Moreover, when Macri took over he issued a decree that transferred regulatory power over the media to Enacom, a newly formed agency heavily influenced by the government. He also signed off on several emergency decrees that reshaped the media landscape, changing aspects of the 2009 Broadcast Media Law. One of the results was the weakening of anti-trust regulations, which led to a further concentration in the hands of the Clarín group (the country's largest media conglomerate) after a merger between its Cablevision and telecommunications giant Telecom.

Argentina still ranks quite highly in international freedom of expressions indexes and is considered a far freer environment for the media than other regional players such as Venezuela, Nicaragua or Mexico.

But Becerra argues that media concentration is damaging: "Excessive concentration damages the diversity of content and restricts the exercise of freedom of expression of other social and political actors," he said.

Where does this leave Argentina's media at the beginning of an electoral process?

Argentines do not trust their media when it comes to politics. According to a 2018 study by the Pew Research Center, only 37% of Argentines believe their news media are reporting the different positions on political issues fairly.

In 2017, only 57% of the population read newspapers, compared with 73% in 2013, says the state-run Cultural Information System of Argentina. At the same time, 70% of the population goes online every day, compared with only 9% in 2013. In 2017, a quarter of the

population got its news from social networks or online portals.

"Traditional media disengaged from their audiences, they did not manage to build a community," said Amado. "This is the perfect breeding ground for Whatsapp groups and 'fake news' on Facebook."

The new media platforms such as Redacción are rising to this challenge, but whether they

MAIN: A man sells newspapers depicting President Mauricio Macri's election victory in Buenos Aires, Argentina, November 2015

CREDIT: Ivan Alvarado/Reuters

will be successful holding power to account and reporting the news as comprehensively as traditional media remains to be seen.

As elections approach, Argentinian media will face a new public test: where will voters go for their news, and how much will this affect the results? For Amado, the challenge to democracy will come from this new, more active model of participation. "Latin America was always marked by a journalism that legitimates power and relates what official sources say," she said. "Now there are more active citizens, for better or for worse." ⊗

Irene Caselli is contributing editor to Index on Censorship, based in Argentina

Eight innovative ways of reporting local news

A global look at how different organisations are responding to the decline of community newspapers

48(01): 18/19 | DOI: 10.1177/0306422019842085

1) USA

VOICE OF SAN DIEGO

What is it? A non-profit news website delivering local investigative journalism and campaigns with an aim "to increase civic participation by giving residents the knowledge and in-depth analysis necessary to become advocates for good government and social progress"
Why? To plug the gap after cutbacks and closures of local papers meant less coverage of important local issues
Who funds it? Sponsors, readers and foundations
Strengths: Its diverse funding model and campaigns on local issues
Potential weaknesses: Relies on a close relationship with the community and an engaged population

2) GUATEMALA

RADIO IXCHEL

What is it? A community radio station with the highest percentage of female participation of any community radio station in the country
Why? Indigenous people were not being represented and even ignored by other stations
Who funds it? NGOs and local people
Strengths: It gives a voice to indigenous local communities, especially women, who are affected by mining and logging industries and whose rights are often abused
Potential weaknesses: Reporting is very dangerous, often women working alone with very little back-up exposing the work of large corporations and corrupt local governments

3) SPAIN

LA VOZ DE GALICIA

What is it? The online service by this established newspaper reports hyperlocal news using special software to curate stories from information gleaned from social media feeds
Why? It provides hyperlocal news without having reporters at every small event or sports fixture
Who funds it? The project is initially being supported by the Google Digital News Initiative
Strengths: A way of letting people know what the news in their area is – including what the football scores are in their very local league
Potential weaknesses: It is fact checked but it sources "news" from individual Twitter and Facebook users who may not be reliable

4) GERMANY

TAGESSPIEGEL LEUTE

What is it? A weekly e-newsletter from daily paper Der Tagesspiegel containing local news for each of Berlin's 12 districts
Why? It fulfils an appetite for hyperlocal news which a city-wide newspaper can't
Who funds it? Advertisers who can target their district
Strengths: A dedicated reporter for each area and a way of letting people know what's happening in their neighbourhood
Potential weaknesses: Richer districts may be better funded and so get more news than less well-off ones. It is not a vehicle for in-depth reporting

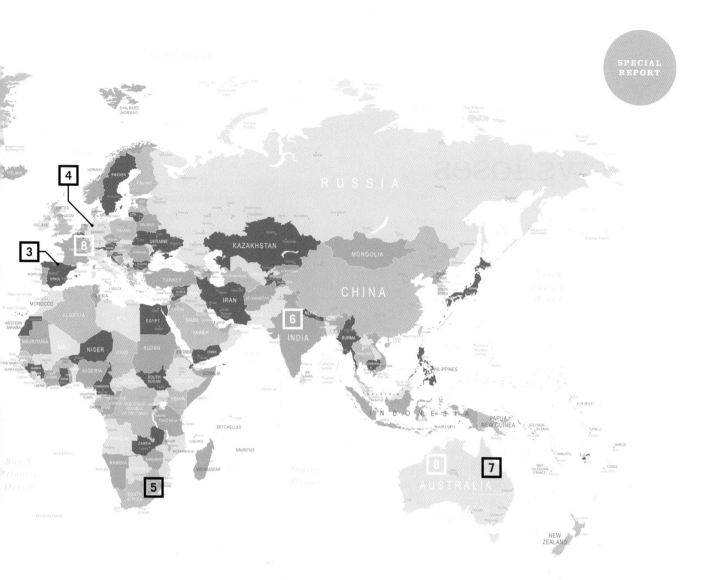

5) SOUTH AFRICA

HASHTAG OUR STORIES

What is it? A social media
organisation telling
global stories from 'people's
perspectives' by curating
videos made on mobile
phones by individuals from
all over the world
Why? To provide an on-the-
ground perspective from
individuals closer to the story
Who funds it? In 2018, the
husband and wife founders
were given $150,000 from
the Los Angeles-based
Snapchat which now owns
part of the company
Strengths: Cheap to oper-
ate. Provides online training
on how to report local
stories with a mobile phone
Potential weaknesses:
Only helps citizens make
video content for social
media platforms. Doesn't
employ journalists

6) INDIA

**CGNET SWARA
(VOICE OF CHHATTISGARH)**

What is it? Local news you
can listen to on a non-smart
mobile phone
Why? It uses citizen journalists to report news from
remote areas where there
is little local news broadcast
in local languages. It also
circumvents a ban on
private radio stations
Who funds it? It is a not-for-
profit organisation which
relies on international trusts
and foundations
Strengths: Broadcasts
news in areas where large
numbers of people are
illiterate and also posts
stories on a global website.
Has been influential nation-
ally and internationally
Potential weaknesses:
Hyperlocal news reporting
with limited coverage

7) QUEENSLAND,
AUSTRALIA

SNIPPETS

What is it? A hyperlocal
news sheet for three
suburbs in the city of
Rockhampton
Why? Local papers were
being swallowed up and the
founder believed local communities were losing out
Who funds it? It is funded
by local businesses that
don't have another outlet
for advertising
Strengths: It is hyperlocal
and making up for the loss
of local papers in parts of
Australia
Potential weaknesses: It is
a one-man band (run by a
retiree) which relies on local
business advertising and
could possibly face conflict
of interest if news is critical
of local business

8) WESTERN EUROPE,
USA AND AUSTRALIA

NEXTDOOR

What is it? A private social
networking service which
puts neighbours in touch
with each other to share
information. It is based in
San Francisco
Why? It was set up in
response to the loss of
newspapers reporting very
local news
Who funds it? A private
company and is valued
at $1.6bn
Strengths: Can be a good
source of certain types of
local news
Potential weaknesses: Mostly covers low-level crime,
lost cats and tips for local
handymen, but more gossip
than reporting. Members in
wealthy Oakland neighbour-
hoods scared of crime were
accused of racial profiling

SOURCES: lavozdegalicia.es/tagesspiegel.de/cgnetswara.org/voiceofsandiego.org | www.scoop.it/Radio Ixchel | ABC.net/Techcrunch/thesouthafrican.com

News loses

"News deserts" are growing in the USA. **Jan Fox** finds 2,000 communities have no daily paper and looks at what is being done to halt the crisis in local news

48(01): 20/22 | DOI: 10.1177/0306422019842087

"**E**VERYONE LOSES WHEN there is no coverage of local politics," said Kate Zernicki, a political reporter at The New York Times, talking about the gradual closing of local news titles across the USA in the past few years.

"It's easier for politicians to get away with things and it's also harder for upcoming new politicians to be heard. Local reporting is how we know what politicians are doing to serve their communities. Without it, we see the reinforcement of the power of money in politics – those who can afford it will run, those who can't will have a hard time getting their messages out.

"I live in New Jersey, where many small papers have been taken over by large chains. You really notice there are not so many local stories, and that's a problem in terms of accountability. We need them."

Referring to a 2013 story about staff of a former Republican governor of New Jersey closing a key road bridge, causing travel chaos, to settle scores with a Democrat mayor, he said: "It was a local paper that broke the Chris Christie and the George Washington Bridge story, for example, and brought it to our attention at the Times."

This year marks 50 years since another important news story was brought to public attention from local sources. In 1969, a young freelance journalist named Seymour Hersh broke the story of the My Lai massacre in Vietnam, one of the biggest atrocities ever perpetrated by the US military. Hersh had trouble getting the story published and eventually took it to Dispatch News Service, a small anti-war news agency in Washington. The story hit the wires on 12 November 1969 and was in newspapers the next day. His book on the massacre would earn Hersh a Pulitzer prize and a job on The New York Times.

Stories like these, with bigger political implications, may have more trouble getting told these days. Of the 3,143 counties in the USA, more than 2,000 now have no daily newspapers and 171 have no newspapers at all, according to the recent University of North Carolina study The Expanding News Desert.

Mike Shapiro runs Tapinto, a network of online local news platforms which operates under a franchise system and has eight million readers in New Jersey, New York, Pennsylvania, South Carolina and Florida. He founded it 10 years ago to combat the loss of local news and the closure of small papers by hedge funds operating on behalf of big newspaper groups.

"Not having a local newspaper undermines democracy," Shapiro told Index. "We tell our franchisees they must run at least one original news story for their town every day and also cover county news, which may be shared with other town papers if relevant.

"In the run-up to local elections, we print weekly statements by candidates in addition to covering debates. This means voters don't have to just depend on a glossy brochure dropped through their doors with very little information on it. We also cover town council meetings, zoning meetings, board of health meetings and so on. Local news is so important for democracy – it's not just about holding government accountable but about more engagement by citizens which, in turn, makes them more informed as voters and encourages them to vote."

This view is borne out by the recent study Financing Dies In Darkness? (The Impact of Newspaper Closures on Public Finance) by Notre Dame's Mendoza Business School, which indicates that newspaper closures are associated with less informed voters and lower voter turnouts.

Shapiro also believes there's an actual financial cost for communities in "local news deserts", particularly when it comes to decisions about local public spending decisions which communities can approve in referendums.

"Bonds are often issued to build schools and other important community buildings, and citizens vote on a bond referendum. If the bond measure passes, key developers are given contracts. Keeping track of how and where that money is spent is important for communities – but if local government isn't scrutinised, it allows corruption to fester," he said.

"In New Jersey there are over 100 municipalities with no local newspaper. Some are economically disadvantaged and so have massive budgets but no press coverage – the local government could be doing a great job with that budget, or not – and not being informed about that is a big problem."

The Notre Dame study also suggests that without local newspapers as watchdogs, local government isn't subject to the same scrutiny from the public on things such as spending.

The lack of local news reporting in the small Los Angeles suburb of Bell allowed corrupt officials, headed by town manager Robert Rizzo, to get away with stealing more than $5 million in public funds by overpaying themselves for years.

A small investigative team from the Los Angeles Times eventually broke the story in 2010, and four years later Rizzo was sentenced to 12 years in jail.

There has perhaps never been a time to worry more about the loss of local news reporting than now. The first few months of 2019 saw a swathe of cuts by digital media and traditional print newspaper groups including Buzzfeed, Verizon Media, Gannet, Vice Media and McClatchy, which has added to the rapid shrinking of local journalism and the further growth of the "news deserts".

It's a phenomenon that has been widely documented in recent years. A Pew Research study indicates that between 2008 and 2017, newspaper newsroom employees declined by 45%, and across all media platforms newsroom employment fell by 23%.

Jeff Jarvis, a former journalist at the Chicago Tribune and New York Daily News, and now professor of journalism at CUNY's Newmark School, says the loss of local journalism is important.

Jarvis sees the issue as a slow evolutionary process. "We are only at the beginning of a long period of disruption and we need to figure [out] how to serve communities," he said. "Only one of our tools is storytelling and communication – we need to think about other →

Local reporting is how we know what politicians are doing to serve their communities

Of the 3,143 counties in the USA, more than 2,000 now have no daily newspaper

→   things like education."

Chris Daggett, former head of the philanthropic Geraldine R Dodge Foundation, has also been trying to figure it out, heading up an experimental incubator lab for local news in New Jersey in partnership with the Knight Foundation and The Democracy Fund. It was, says Daggett, who stepped down from the role last year, largely unsuccessful.

"We were trying to find the next business model to make local news work, but after eight years we failed. ProPublica [a non-profit newsroom with a focus on investigative journalism] has done good work but they are not exactly knocking the lights out. Tapinto is doing some

interesting stuff with their franchise model, but on the whole it's hard to get revenue," he said.

"Local reporting is vital for democracy, but I think there is also a kind of laziness in the electorate right now and they don't want local journalism until they need it. A reporter finds out something and then suddenly they are interested. The rise of Trump did see newspaper subscriptions go up as people saw a need for in-depth journalism."

Zernicki believes the loss of local reporting is a problem also for young journalists who, like her, used to cut their teeth at the local level. "It was where you honed your instincts – a wonderful training ground," she said. "And it was local papers that used to bring talent to the nationals. We don't have time to nurture those skills." ⊗

Jan Fox is the US contributing editor for Index on Censorship. She is based in Los Angeles

THE LITTLE NEWSPAPER THAT DEFINITELY COULD

||||||||||||||||||||||||||||||||||||||||||||||||||||

There's a quiet revolution in local journalism going on in the small town of Vale, Oregon – population 1,900 – where LES ZAINTZ runs the weekly paper, the Malheur Enterprise.

ZAINTZ, WHO IS both editor and publisher, bought it in 2015 when he retired from The Oregonian, a Portland daily where he was twice nominated for a Pulitzer prize. No one could be more surprised at what's happened since, and he has a delightfully self-deprecating sense of humour about it all.

"Why did I buy it? Well, I'm not very smart!" he said. "It was a terrible paper so we could buy it for next to nothing."

His intent was to preserve the paper, which had been founded in 1909, saying: "The fuel was the heating up of the 2016 elections and the 'fake media' storm. I thought we could buy it and run it as a kind of journalism laboratory where we could attack erosion and trust in the media, and it

became a mission."

With a staff of two reporters, one delivery lady in her 70s and an office cat, the Malheur Enterprise embarked on a path that Zaintz calls "relentlessly local".

When Zaintz bought the paper it had a circulation of 700. Now it has 20,000 unique readers per week in print and online issues throughout Malheur County.

"We don't do clickbait, we don't do high school sports. We cover real news and put the spotlight on community issues and solutions. We've proved that the public is hungry for real local news about substantive issues," said Zaintz.

"Malheur County is 30% Latino and they are very under-represented in the power structure and in the media. We've also struggled to recruit foster parents here for children who have been removed from homes where there is drug abuse. Or we have to deal with the homeless. These issues need the media spotlight on them or the community will find it much harder to come up with solutions."

The Malheur Enterprise covers local news so well that in 2018 it became the first weekly paper to be awarded the prestigious Investigative Reporters and Editors Freedom of Information award for a story about a criminal who had faked his mental health issues.

The result of the award is that ProPublica is now funding a third full-time journalist to work on that story for a year, and Zaintz will take on two interns this summer.

Turks retreat online for news

Turkey is the world's leading jailer of journalists and most media toes the government line. As **Kaya Genç** reports, independent local reporters now use Twitter and Facebook to publish stories

48(01): 23/25 | DOI: 10.1177/0306422019842088

AT ABOUT 9AM every day, editors from Bia, an Istanbul-based news portal, walk out to the street to have a break for coffee and cigarettes. Around the same time, thousands check Bianet.org, their website, to get their morning briefing, which mixes local dispatches with thoughtful pieces of reportage in both Turkish and English.

Bia's humble headquarters in the city's Beyoğlu neighbourhood resembles that of a small newspaper. Established with funding from the European Union, Bia, which stands for Bağımsız İletişim Ağı (Independent Communication Network), serves as a pool into which locally reported news from Turkish cities flow.

Since Bia was started 18 years ago, local media in Turkey has followed a global trend and struggled for survival. This, for a time, made Bia's model and patronage increasingly vital for the future of Turkish journalism. But with the advent of social media and the mass imprisonment of journalists, opposition-leaning Turks are more likely to get their news directly from the Twitter and Facebook accounts of trusted correspondents, and Bia is struggling.

Local newspapers are in real trouble in Turkey. In October 2018, as the Turkish lira lost one third of its value against the dollar, seven local newspapers in Izmir, Turkey's third largest city, announced they would no longer be publishing issues on Sundays and Özgür Ses, a local daily paper with a 14-year history, announced it would become a weekly.

All around the country, the rising price of paper has forced publications to reduce the number of pages, and many page designers and reporters have been laid off.

Expenses have increased by 150%, advertising revenues have fallen by 25% and some 900 local papers have closed since 2014. Only around 1,000 survive.

A lot of reporters have also been imprisoned by the government. Figures released by independent journalism platform P24 show at least 160 media workers are in prison in Turkey today, making the country the world's leading jailer of journalists. Among those imprisoned are local reporters chronicling the violence between Kurdish militias and Turkish security forces in eastern Turkey. Other journalists have had to leave the country.

These troubles in local news are part of a larger crisis in Turkish journalism.

Over the past half-decade, mainstream Turkish media have largely caved in to state intimidation. Most newspapers toe the government line and others have gone out of business or have been forcibly shut down. This restrictive atmosphere allowed independent portals such as Bia to flourish.

The project originally emerged as a response to what Bia editors described as "the professional downfall" of mainstream Turkish media during the 1990s and out of a need "for real news sources for social opposition".

"In its inception, Bia started an initiative to strengthen local media," Haluk Kalafat, Bia's co-editor, told Index. "Our goal was to slightly alter the centralist nature of Turkish journalism. We wanted to get proper news from local sources."

Turks are more likely to get their news directly from the Twitter and Facebook accounts of trusted correspondents

CREDIT: Osman Orsal/Reuters

ABOVE: Demonstrators protest the arrest of two prominent journalists in Istanbul, Turkey, November 2015. The newspaper headline reads: "Black day for the press"

To this end, Bia conducted education seminars and partnered with local papers and journalists. But Kalafat's team now faces a new challenge as social media increasingly leaves its local reporting capabilities in the shade.

The Press Advertisement Institution, the authority which distributes official advertisements to newspapers, noticed the change and asked all local papers to become digital. Its president said he preferred "a total conversion" to digital and said 2019 would be the year of digital local journalism. He said this was also "the wish of [the] Turkish presidency".

His comments showed how the general decline of local news, similar to what is happening in countries including Britain and the USA, also served a political purpose. Sacking reporters and "turning digital" to save local journalism – and with the lofty aim of

modernising news – is, in fact, playing into the hands of the government.

That digital trend may benefit young local reporters who use social media, but it also endangers Bia's model, which is based on journalism from first-hand sources processed with rigorous editing in the Istanbul office. As an outcome, reporters rather than editors now drive the news cycle.

İsmail Saymaz, a leading investigative reporter, has 1.2 million Twitter followers, a figure larger than the followers of Radikal, the paper he worked for until its closure in 2014. Pelin Ünker, who was the Turkish member of the reporting team that broke the Panama Papers story and who won a Pulitzer Prize in 2017, has a more modest Twitter following, but while propaganda snippets of pro-government titles don't make any waves, readers engage with the kind of investigative journalism she provides.

Ünker is freelancing these days, and many young reporters who emerged in the past five years follow in her steps. They may have no outlet other than Twitter, and no editorial input for their dispatches, but these only fuel their identification as local reporters.

Ece Temelkuran hosted a TV show, wrote a popular newspaper column and published novels before she was laid off in 2013 over a critical article. She has since built a massive following on Twitter, where her 2.6 million followers rely on her posts to get an opposition perspective on Turkey.

"Social media definitely makes it easier for the journalist and the reader to meet up," Temelkuran told Index, but the disappearance of editorial oversight troubles her. "The lack of editing is horrible. [The] written word requires a second look before it is published or posted. Many consider this an unnecessary filter. I think they are not aware how powerful words can be and how irreversible some mistakes may be."

Now living in Croatia, she believes Turkish local news faces numerous challenges. "The biggest challenge is the same as it has been in the old days: proximity," she said. "The source, the reader and the journalist live too close to each other. There are no institutional barriers to protect the journalist from the reader and those who would be intimidated, or challenged, by the news. This has been the problem of local journalists all along. But with the false intimacy that social media creates, the problem seems to be more challenging than ever."

Not long ago, Temelkuran edited a Turkish opposition newspaper, BirGün, where she worked with local reporters. "Things for Turkish media were not yet as bad as they are today," she said. "But I remember writing in 2011 that all the Turkish respected journalists will end up in social media. That prediction, unfortunately, more or less came true."

She added: "Being the editor of an opposition paper for a short while made me think about [the] prospects of journalism in Turkey from a different perspective. Especially in such outlets, journalism in Turkey today depends on personal

Among the imprisoned are local reporters chronicling the violence between Kurdish militias and Turkish security forces in eastern Turkey

sacrifice and [the daring] of the journalists. Financially, only young people who don't have children can afford the burden of not getting paid properly. The staff is renewed constantly [and] this leaves the news outlets with incredibly enthusiastic, yet less experienced, journalists. That in itself causes problems in terms of sustainable credibility of the news outlet."

Kalafat, the Bia editor, says people mostly follow its website for long-form features and commentary. Readers interested in developing local news, meanwhile, will "naturally go to social media accounts providing live feeds, or to Instagram accounts of photography initiatives, like Nar Photos, whose quality of photography they trust".

This sounds like an admission of defeat if the social media of reporters has now become the primary source of local news while Bia is shifting its focus to human rights journalism. This way, the concern for getting local news right appears to morph into a concern for getting broader issues right, including the environment and human rights.

Bia's main page now presents new sections: Human Rights Reports, EU Accession, Unemployed Journalists Chasing News and Male Violence Monitoring.

"[The] internet changes methods of journalism, but its fundamental values remain mostly the same," Kalafat said, emphasising that if journalists uphold those values, local news can still thrive as a composite of sites such as Bia and vigorous reporting on social media. ⊗

Kaya Genç is a contributing editor for Index on Censorship, based in Istanbul

48(01): 26/27 | DOI: 10.1177/0306422019842089

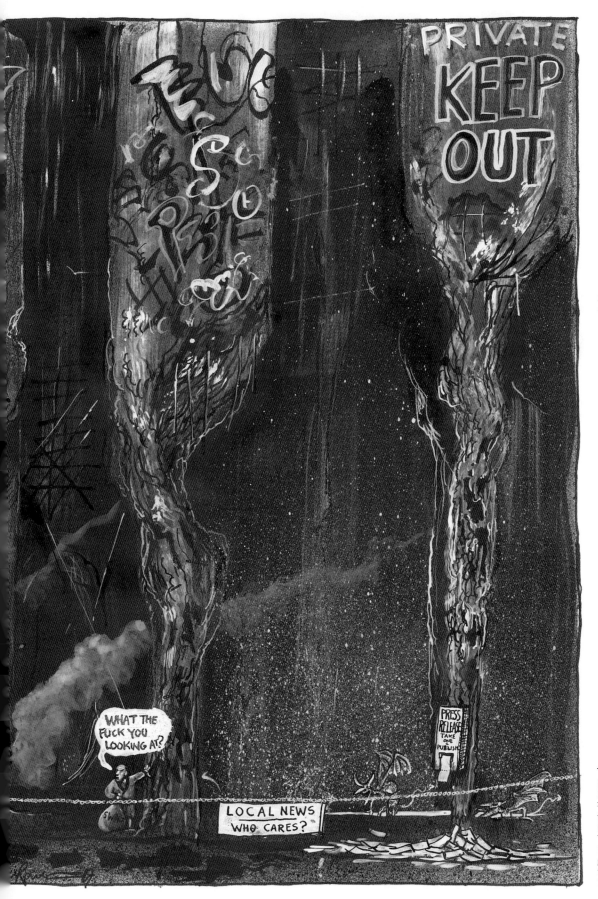

SPECIAL
REPORT

MARTIN ROWSON
is a cartoonist for
The Guardian and
the author of various
books, including
The Communist
Manifesto (2018), a
graphic novel adap-
tion of the famous
19th century book

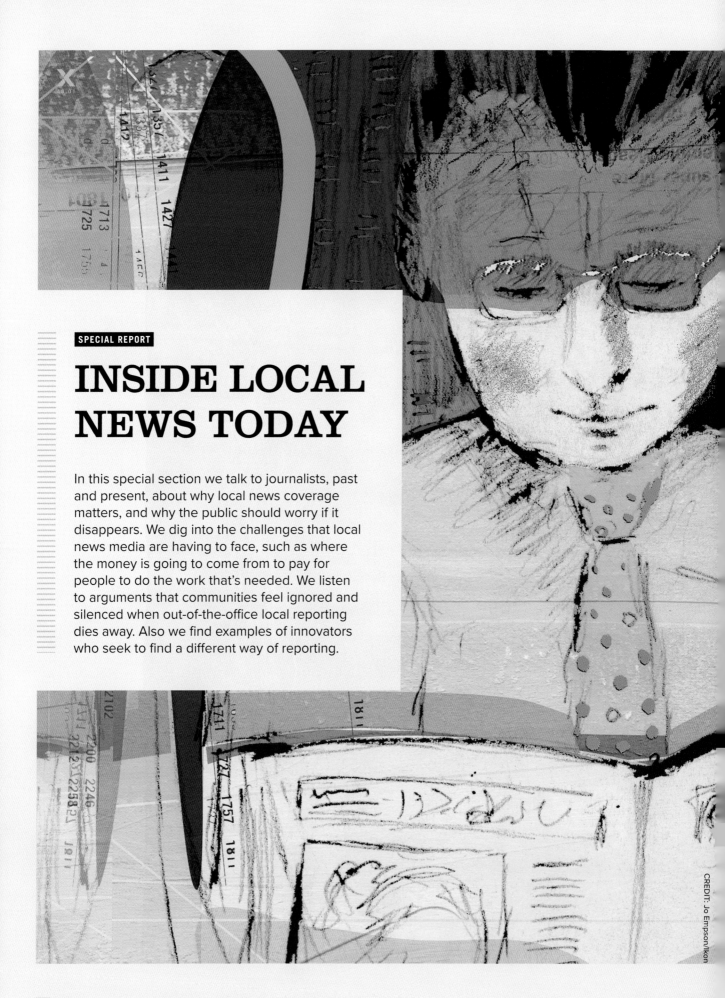

INSIDE LOCAL NEWS TODAY

In this special section we talk to journalists, past and present, about why local news coverage matters, and why the public should worry if it disappears. We dig into the challenges that local news media are having to face, such as where the money is going to come from to pay for people to do the work that's needed. We listen to arguments that communities feel ignored and silenced when out-of-the-office local reporting dies away. Also we find examples of innovators who seek to find a different way of reporting.

INSIDE LOCAL NEWS

What happens when our local news disappears?

After three decades in local journalism, **Tracey Bagshaw** investigates the state of UK regional news today. What she finds is disturbing. Newspapers are closing and reporters are no longer covering local courts and councils

48(01): 29/31 I DOI:10.1177/0306422019842090

LOCAL NEWSPAPERS IN the UK are in big trouble. They have seen their budgets slashed and staff numbers cut while others have disappeared completely.

The National Union of Journalists warned in 2016 that the regional newspaper industry was in "freefall", saying that the number of regional journalists had halved to about 6,500, with centralised newsrooms, leaving press benches in many council chambers and courtrooms empty.

Meanwhile, a study by Press Gazette, a trade publication, in 2018 found that 228 local titles had closed since 2005, 40 of those in 2017.

Even where newspapers still exist, journalists increasingly have their work cut out to keep "worthy" content on the agenda, and find →

The most read story on the Gloucester Live site in 2018 was a lump of wood floating on the River Severn which "could" have been a monster

The result is a handful of reporters rushing to produce the maximum number of stories in the least possible time. Hence court and local council reporting is deemed not time efficient

→ coverage of local councils and courts competing with click-friendly online snippets which create big digital audiences. The most read story on the Gloucester Live site in 2018 was a lump of wood floating on the River Severn which "could" have been a monster.

A story count over five days in the Norfolk local paper, the Eastern Daily Press, in January 2019, found 37 council-related stories, 23 court stories and four inquests in papers. The same period in 2009 had 51 local government stories, 27 court cases and eight inquests.

Many local newspapers no longer have lobby correspondents in Westminster. The EDP once had three but now the role is held by a Norwich-based reporter in addition to her other responsibilities. Fewer newspapers have reporters in crown courts every day, and local government meetings are more of a stretch to cover than they used to be.

Current EDP editor David Powles recognises there are problems but said: "There's no denying our newsrooms are smaller than they once were but... coverage of councils, court and local organisations remains at the heart of what we do."

His 15-strong Norwich newsroom (backed up by feature writers, digital and sport reporters, and about 20 reporters in seven district offices) maintains specialists in business, local government health, crime, education and court.

But when all local newspapers are under enormous pressure to make cutbacks, something has to give.

In January 2018, journalism students at the University of the West of England observed Bristol Magistrates' Court for a week. They said it took three days before they spotted a reporter and said the majority of the 240 cases

they sat in on went unreported. Most reports that did appear came from Crown Prosecution Service handouts.

They concluded that with about 300 magistrates' courts in England and Wales, it was possible that 15,000 newsworthy stories were potentially being missed every week.

Journalist Paul Cheston retired in 2016 after three decades covering court cases for the London Evening Standard.

He told Index: "The collapse of local paper circulation has led to reduced costs, reduced pagination, reduced staff levels and training reduced to practically nothing. The result is a handful of reporters rushing to produce the maximum number of stories in the least possible time. Hence court and local council reporting is deemed not time efficient.

"Trying to cobble together a story from court lists, police press releases and, even worse, social media just because there was no reporter in court to take down what happened as it happened is not only plain wrong but dangerous. Apart from the potential inaccuracies, the subsequent report loses all privilege because it runs the risk of being neither fair, accurate nor contemporaneous."

In Lancashire, David Graham, who worked for the Lancashire Evening Telegraph in the 1960s and 1970s has also noticed the changes.

"The area magistrates' court, a goldmine for news, sat on Monday and Thursday, with a juvenile court every couple of weeks on a Tuesday, and these were often staffed by two of us, so we could take it in turns to nip back to the office and file copy," he said. "The local weekly papers also sent reporters and there were often three or four of us on the press bench at any one time, sharing notes and covering for each other."

They shared a retiring room with police, lawyers and court officials, gathering plenty of background and local gossip. "That sort of contact can never be replicated with a phone call to a court office to get a list of cases and verdicts," he said. "Magistrates and solicitors were often local councillors as well, so again there was regular crossover contact, with bits of information you could never hope to pick up remotely."

RIGHT: A newspaper stall selling Brighton's local newspaper The Argus in the city's railway station, UK

With a wide patch and several titles to cover, a news editor at one regional media group told Index that his reporters covered as many council meetings and court sittings as possible, but that there were new obstacles.

"The role of grassroots local journalism is more important than ever as we face the combination of public bodies with highly paid marketing teams trying to manipulate the news, and people on community social media sites sharing information, which is often false," he said. "We increasingly find that councils, health trusts, education trusts and emergency services are more combative in protecting their image and attempting to steer us away from certain issues and stories."

In 2016 a report by the Centre for the Study of Media, Communication and Power at King's College, London found UK towns where daily local newspapers had shut suffered from a "democracy deficit", with reduced community engagement and increased distrust of public bodies.

Martin Moore, director of the centre, and one of the authors, told the BBC: "We can all have our own social media account, but when [local papers] are depleted or in some cases simply don't exist, people lose a communal voice. They feel angry, not listened to and more likely to believe malicious rumours. Because it's not necessarily the sexy stuff, like big investigations, for quite some time people didn't notice it was disappearing."

Councils say they want transparency, and to this end some are becoming more pro-active. Norfolk County Council is planning to feature its meetings live on YouTube, and local politicians across the UK live tweet from meetings and send copies of their speeches to reporters.

But nothing replaces having reporters in the room, which is why about 150 local democracy reporters (LDRs) are employed through a new collaboration between the BBC and local newsrooms solely to cover local authorities.

One of these LDRs is Neil McGrory, a journalist with 18 years' experience, who covers East Dunbartonshire and North Lanarkshire

councils in Scotland. Since June 2018, McGrory has filed more than 230 local council stories for print and online.

Google and Facebook are now the largest distributors of news. Neither company employs trained journalists, but Facebook is launching a £4.5 million training scheme that will pay for 80 community journalists to improve coverage. The scheme will be run in tandem with the major UK media groups and is designed to fill the gaps.

But some local titles are proudly fighting to maintain the depth of their local reporting.

Sinead Corr co-founded the weekly Stortford Independent in Essex with backing from an independent publisher, and has made a conscious decision to concentrate on local news.

"I go to every single town council meeting," Corr said. "My colleague attends every parish council meeting in the other part of our patch... We keep a similar watching brief for county council matters. Because I attend every town council meeting, the members make a point of telling me what's going on and most of them [also] serve at district and/or county level."

As EDP editor Powles said: "How could people make their informed choices about who is best to run their local services if they are not able to get a neutral account as to what it is exactly they do?" ⊗

Tracey Bagshaw has worked in local newspapers for 30 years, as a reporter, news editor and chief sub-editor on a regional daily title

INSIDE LOCAL NEWS

Slip sliding away

Former local reporters **Andrew Morton**, **Julie Posetti** and **Richard Littlejohn** reflect on what happens when news is not covered any more

48(01): 32/35 | DOI: 10.1177/0306422019842092

"THEY DIDN'T STAY SECRET FOR LONG"

WHEN I STARTED out as a trainee reporter on a provincial weekly newspaper 48 years ago, the first port of call on a Monday morning was the local police station.

Over a cup of tea, the desk sergeant would let us browse through the overnight crime ledger – burglaries, road accidents, who'd been nicked for being drunk and disorderly...

From there, it was on to the fire station and the ambulance headquarters for a daily update on everything from a chip pan fire to a sudden death.

We could wander into the town hall and talk to anyone.

The part-time council leader was an engine driver who didn't own a car. He lived near me and I used to give him a lift to committee meetings in the office van. He'd fill me in on the latest gossip and let me flick through the minutes.

All committees were open to the press and the public. If there were any secrets, or dodgy back-door planning deals, they didn't stay secret for long.

Like Marlon Brando, we covered the waterfront. The city's population was just 80,000, but it supported one weekly paper, one twice-weekly paper (Tuesdays and Fridays) and a six-day-a-week evening paper. Reporters were assigned full-time to local magistrates, assizes and civil courts – we'd even cover small parish councils.

When I graduated to Birmingham, and latterly Fleet Street, the drill was much the same, if even more intense. Newspapers could afford specialist correspondents, with encyclopaedic knowledge of their own patches.

Pubs and afternoon drinking clubs served as information exchanges. There was one, in particular, near the Houses of Parliament, where journalists, coppers, spooks, politicians, trades unionists, known gangsters and men of the cloth would all congregate.

Everyone knew the boundaries, but all appreciated the value of somewhere they could chat, off the record. When I was an industrial correspondent, most of my business was done over a pint of beer.

It is often claimed that today, thanks to social media, we are better informed. Not true.

What we get from the internet is a bombardment of rumour, speculation, vile abuse and what we have come to know as "fake news". Citizen journalism is no such thing. It's activist-driven and devoid of the rigour required of proper journalists.

Old-school newspaper hacks had to get their facts right or they'd quickly get found out.

But they broke important stories, backed by hard evidence. It's often said, to cite one example, that if there'd been a proper neighbourhood reporter in west London, the problems at Grenfell Tower would have been exposed long before the tragic fire which claimed so many innocent lives.

Sadly, local papers have been put out of business as classified advertising has migrated to the internet. The rot also set in when councils merged and moved their headquarters miles away from the people they are paid to serve. These new supersized local authorities started holding their meetings in camera. Some of them launched their own newspapers to peddle partisan political propaganda and withdrew advertising from independent papers in an attempt to stifle hostile, or at least inconvenient, reporting.

Despite freedom of information laws, we now live in a much more secretive era. Civil servants have been fined, and jailed, for selling stories to newspapers, even though they were undeniably in the public interest.

Reporters have been dragged before the courts for allegedly bribing contacts in the police and government, although pretty much all these cases have been thrown out by sensible juries.

When I started in this game, giving a bottle of Scotch to the desk sergeant at the local nick every Christmas was considered good manners. These days, it would be a criminal offence.

Over the past 12 years, the number of frontline journalists in Britain has fallen from 23,000 to 17,000. Local papers have gone to the wall. The city where I began my career, Peterborough, boasts a population now of 196,000. But it has only one, weekly, newspaper.

Crimes, courts, dodgy deals at the town hall – these all go unreported. This isn't just a tragedy for journalists, it's a disaster for our democracy.

*Daily Mail columnist **Richard Littlejohn** started his career on the Peterborough Standard*

OPPOSITE: A street stall selling the Ipswich Star. The newspaper based in Suffolk, UK, saw its circulation drop by 37% year on year in 2018

WHY SHOULD WE CARE ABOUT LOCAL JOURNALISM?

"

Most daily papers in Germany suffer from a shrinking circulation. That's mainly due to an ageing readership: the old die, the young look at their mobiles. As if that wasn't enough, advertising revenues are shrinking dramatically as well. Who wants to search the paper for a new house, car or holiday when all of that is just one mouse-click away?

Despite all that, Germany still has one of the highest densities worldwide of local papers, with very loyal readers. The reason is not news about Donald Trump or Justin Trudeau, Venezuela or Vietnam. National and international news is covered by TV and radio as well

as being ubiquitous on the web. What keeps papers afloat is their local and regional news.

Local competence counts. Events on people's doorsteps are often not found via Google. Why is the local nursery closed? Why have the church bells stopped ringing? Are the roadworks on the main road ever going to stop? Those questions are answered by only the local paper.

No doubt printed newspapers will become a rarity in five or 10 years' time. But slowing down, or even stopping, the decline will work only with local news.

RALF GUNKEL is editor at Stuttgarter Zeitung and in charge of 10 district editions specialising in local news

"

"IT WAS THE BEGINNING OF A LONG PERIOD OF DECLINE"

I BEGAN MY JOURNALISM career in the late 1980s in the regional Australian working-class city of Wollongong, just an hour down the road from Sydney. It was a story-rich industrial town – think big corporate polluters, paedophile mayors, a corrupt local council and a string of macabre murders. A place where many prominent national reporters had "cut their teeth".

I was a trainee journalist in what was then a scrappy commercial radio newsroom. There were five reporters at Radio 2 Double O, as it was known when I joined in 1989, pushing out five-minute local news bulletins every 30 to 60 minutes from 5am to 7pm. We worked in what was effectively a bi-media newsroom (long before the days of multimedia journalism), collaborating with colleagues from the co-owned WIN TV News, who sat adjacent to us. And we competed in a diverse pre-internet media landscape.

This was a city of about 150,000 people served by a campaigning Fairfax Media title called the Illawarra Mercury, which then had capacity for high-impact local investigative reporting; two well-staffed commercial radio newsrooms; a regional Australian Broadcasting Corporation station with a solid, if somewhat antiquated, newsroom; and three fully staffed commercial TV news services covering a suite of beats. Every Monday night, for example, Wollongong City Council meetings were covered by a full deck of local media representatives.

This was a historic highpoint in media diversity for the region and the competition was mostly healthy. But it was also possibly unsustainable. And it was the beginning of a long period of decline.

But this is not just another story about the slow death of local journalism. It's a story about local journalism's diminished capacity to carry out accountability reporting at a time when democracy is more fragile than it's been in almost a century.

As a teenage trainee journalist at 2 Double O, now known as i98fm, I was warned to beware of the sexually predatory Wollongong mayor and state parliamentarian Frank Arkell. I quickly learned that this man was not just a vulgar harasser but was also reputedly part of a paedophile ring that had operated in the city for decades, and had deep links to local government, the Catholic church and the regional business community. It sounds like a conspiracy theory, right?

Wrong. Arkell was eventually exposed by the Illawarra Mercury as a prominent member of a paedophile ring. Not long afterwards, he was brutally murdered by a man who claimed to have been one of his victims.

Fast-forward a decade and Wollongong City Council was sacked by the state government in the midst of a scandal – again exposed by the Illawarra Mercury – involving sexual favours exchanged for development approvals

Today, the population of Wollongong is burgeoning, but the media landscape has contracted dramatically – despite the arrival of digital media. Two commercial radio stations produce a limited number of news bulletins that rarely break news and sound more like audio press releases. There is now only one, poorly-staffed, local TV news service that does its best with an oily rag. And the utterly depleted Illawarra Mercury is up for sale following the ignominious end of the 185-year-old Fairfax Media brand. The ABC, at least, has expanded its regional presence and airtime but its local content has limited mainstream audience impact.

Local news is often regarded as a training ground for journalists and looked down on by big city or national news organisations. But without robust, well-resourced

Without robust, well-resourced local news services, my home town would likely never have learned of a depraved, destructive abuse of power that underpinned a paedophile ring

local news services, my home town would likely never have learned of the depraved, destructive abuse of power that underpinned a decades-old paedophile ring intertwined with a corrupt city council. Nor would it have learned of the illegal disposal of potentially cancer-causing chemicals down mineshafts by industrial polluters. Nor would it have known about allegations of waterfront corruption.

When I returned to Wollongong as a journalism academic in 2013, two decades after I left the local ABC bureau to work on a national ABC TV programme, I found little evidence of the feisty, robust local journalism tradition that birthed me as a reporter. Now, despite the power of social media and the ability of online communities to mobilise, I fear that the paedophile mayor would find it much easier to keep his cover in 2019.

As we continue to search for sustainable business models to support independent journalism that truly holds power to account and counters propaganda, we cannot afford to sacrifice the "local".

*Now at Oxford University's Reuters Institute for the Study of Journalism, **Julie Posetti** started her career on radio station 2 Double O, New South Wales, Australia*

CREDIT: (Posetti) Tim Anger; (Morton) Ken Lennox

BEING THE EYES AND EARS OF THE COMMUNITY

RHYTHM AND ROUTINE. That was the general maxim for life on a local newspaper. It was where I cut my teeth – or rather my indentures – as a thrusting young journalist working on several weeklies in Plymouth, Truro and Tavistock in the south-west of England.

From memory, Mondays would be visits to the local police station and magistrates' court, which invariably yielded a yarn; Tuesday would be a trip to the council planning department; Wednesday was the weekly council meeting; and Thursday meant a call on the local butcher – who was also the mayor of the Devon market town of Tavistock – to drum up a story. As a budding reporter, I quickly realised that the word "row" always helped propel a thin story on to the front page. Saturdays meant standing outside the register office interviewing several happy couples and dreaming up headlines other than "Dance led to Romance" or "Met in a Pub".

The extended stints on local newspapers was part of our training on the Mirror Group graduate scheme, which was based in Plymouth. Former luminaries include military historian Patrick Bishop, investigative journalist Nick Davies, crime writer Val McDermid and former Prime Minister Tony Blair's right-hand man, Alastair Campbell.

Early on, we were taught to distinguish between human interest stories – essentially births, marriages and deaths – and public importance stories which were, in the main, the ruminations of the local council and other official bodies. The boring but important stuff.

Parachuted into local communities, we were encouraged to look around for "off diary" stories, to be the eyes and ears of the community. So I would regularly drive round the area just looking around. It was a routine that yielded dividends.

I remember spotting a man in his driveway who was building a concrete yacht. He told me that once it was finished he planned to sail to Australia. I wonder what happened to him.

On a Plymouth council estate, a couple of houses next door to one another caught my eye. It was clear that the occupants had spent thousands of pounds on improvements that made their homes stand out from the humdrum surroundings.

A knock on the door revealed that they were the first in their road to take advantage of Prime Minister Margaret Thatcher's controversial sale of local authority housing.

Other features of the weekly journalistic routine in the 1970s would not pass modern muster. When I worked on the Sunday Independent at its branch office in Truro, one of my jobs was to find a pretty local girl who would agree to be pictured for the newspaper. This wasn't some topless Page Three Girl made famous by Rupert Murdoch's Sun but a winsome portrait of a young woman carrying, say, a basket of daffodils.

I duly spotted a young woman working in a local antiques shop. She seemed to have all the qualities needed to brighten up an inside page.

I strolled back to the office and informed my senior reporter, a chap called Paul Mann, who is now a successful novelist.

He wanted to double-check my choice so he gave her the once over. He took one look at the young lady in question and shook his head. "Nahh, mate, she's too old."

We later discovered that the "ancient" shop assistant, then in her early 30s, was none other than model Jean Shrimpton, the face of the Swinging Sixties and regularly described as the most beautiful woman in the world. For a time she quietly ran a hotel in the nearby town of Penzance. That was one "human interest" scoop that got away.

Of course so much has changed since those days –

We later discovered that the "ancient" shop assistant... was none other than model Jean Shrimpton

---

but much has remained the same.

Looking at the Tavistock Times – now the amalgamated Tavistock Times Gazette – the content has barely changed; tragic road traffic accidents, shoddy builders and planning rows. That word again.

Ownership has changed hands: the Tavvy, as it was known, is now run by the local newspaper group founded by Sir Ray Tindle, who earned his knighthood by saving dozens of local newspapers from extinction.

While the online revolution has cut a daunting swathe through the ranks of local newspapers – the NUJ has called for an inquiry into local newspaper provision – new technology has made mini-Murdochs of us all.

Six years ago, my former Mirror Group colleague Keith Wheatley set up his own online journal, Around Wellington, to keep everyone in his Somerset town up to date on local events. January this year was his most popular month to date.

His enterprise is no money spinner, but Keith keeps his head above water – and still manages to get the word "row" into his planning reports.

*Celebrity author and royal biographer **Andrew Morton** started his career on various weekly newspapers in the south-west of England*

INSIDE LOCAL NEWS

Who will do the difficult stories now?

Index editor **Rachael Jolley** reports on why local UK editors fear a future where politicians and other powerful figures are not held to account

48(01): 36/39 I DOI: 10.1177/0306422019842093

AROUND 97% OF senior journalists and editors of the UK's regional newspapers and news sites say they are worried that local newspapers do not have the resources to hold power to account in the way that they did in the past, according to a survey carried out by the Society of Editors and Index on Censorship.

And 70% of those surveyed are very worried about this (see Question 3).

OPPOSITE: A journalist records video on a mobile phone as former Chief Inspector Sir Norman Bettison gives a statement outside Preston Crown Court, 2018

QUESTION ONE

In terms of percentage of local news stories, how much less local news do you feel is getting reported in your area than 10 years ago?

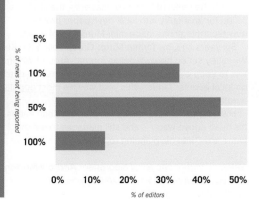

% of news not being reported

% of editors

QUESTION TWO

Does your news operation cover crown and magistrates court cases?

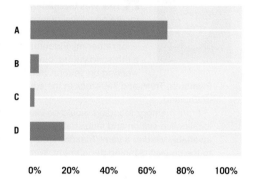

KEY

A On a weekly basis we carry a story about a case
B At least once a month
C A couple of times per year
D Hardly ever

The survey, carried out earlier this year, asked for responses from senior journalists and current and former editors working in regional journalism. It was part of work carried out for this magazine to discover the biggest challenges ahead for local journalists.

It follows steady declines in regional newspaper sales and online audiences in recent years. Figures from the Audit Bureau of Circulation for 2018 showed many regional papers suffering steep declines in readership, including the Cambridge News (34% down year-on-year to only 7,124 copies), the Ipswich Star (37% down) and morning daily The Scotsman (17% down).

The survey found that 50% of editors and journalists are most worried that no one will be doing the difficult stories in future (see Q5), and 43% that the public's right to know will disappear. A small number worry most that there will be too much emphasis on light, funny stories.

There are some specific issues that editors worry about, such as covering court cases and council meetings with limited resources.

Michael Sassi, editor of the Nottingham Post and the Nottingham Live website, told Index: "There's no doubt that local decision-makers aren't subject to the level of scrutiny they once were. There are large numbers of councils right across the country – making big decisions involving millions of pounds of public money – who may never see a local reporter. Many local authorities will be operating in the knowledge that no one will ever ask them an awkward question. Which, obviously enough, does nothing to help build trust in local democracy.

"Just because it's hard to persuade local audiences to read about what their elected representatives are doing in their name, local publishers haven't given up. Most – including the Nottingham Post – still believe that it's part of their job to take the issues that are important for local people (and for local democracy) and to find ways of making these issues interesting and readable."

He added that there were now far fewer staff reporters writing about local councils than there were 15 years ago, but pointed to projects such as the BBC-backed local democracy reporters as one way of giving papers more resources.

"Certainly, Nottingham's local democracy reporter Kit Sandeman – who is based in our newsroom – has been able to go to many of the council meetings that we'd previously had to drop," he said. "He religiously works his way through agendas, builds old-style relationships with local politicians and turns up important stories that may never have come to light."

Overall, editors seem far more concerned than the wider public that reducing local reporting could create increasing democratic unaccountability (see p39).

Twenty editors surveyed say that they feel only half as much local news is getting covered in their area compared with a decade earlier (see Q1), with 15 respondents saying that about 10% less news is getting covered. And 74% say their news outlet covers court cases once a week, and 18% say they hardly ever cover courts.

Around 70% (32 respondents) say in areas where the local newspaper has closed down the public know less about what was going on. Only two respondents feel alternative news sources have sprung up.

The survey went out to members of the Society of Editors. Their membership includes former and current editors, deputy editors and managing editors of local newspapers →

QUESTION THREE

Do you worry that local papers don't have the resources to hold power to account in the way they did in the past?

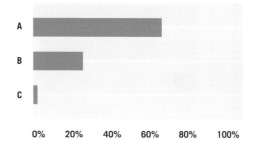

KEY

A I worry a lot
B I worry a little
C I don't think this is an issue

→ around the UK. Forty five responses to the survey were received.

Commenting on the survey, Ian Murray, director of the Society of Editors, said: "There's real danger of local communities almost sleepwalking into this situation where you would have a cabal of people running the politics in town. That's a real step backwards to where, [as] in the past, somewhere is run by the local aristocracy."

He added that in many places, losing their local newspaper or radio station was going to "damage the local community's soul". Murray, who was previously the editor of the Southern Daily Echo, said he felt that many people were disengaged from their local communities and would worry only when something affected them.

Communities who had lost their local news media were left dependent on magazines funded by local authorities, which covered only a certain amount of information, and on "the Twitterati". Local democracy was vitally important, with "decisions being made in your name". If fewer people were watching what was going on, there would be fewer people

QUESTION FOUR

In areas where local newspapers have closed down, I think:

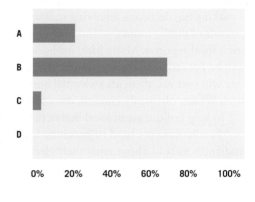

KEY

A Local politicians have too much power
B The public knows less about what is happening
C Other alternatives have sprung up
D Something else

making decisions on local budgets, he said.

But not everyone is gloomy about the future. One senior journalist added: "While it's right to be concerned about the future provision of local news and capacity to hold the powerful to account, tackle challenging stories and maintain the public's right to know, we shouldn't succumb to the belief that this vital sector is doomed. Plenty of bright, young, well-trained journalists are still entering the industry at this grassroots level and new initiatives, like those backed by the BBC and Facebook, are breathing in new life."

Meanwhile, one local editor told the survey that more relevant news was being covered now than a decade ago, but added: "I fear that opinion is prized more than fact, and comfortable narratives are more acceptable than open-ended, campaigning journalism." ⊗

Rachael Jolley is the editor of Index on Censorship

QUESTION FIVE

My biggest fear about the future of local news is:

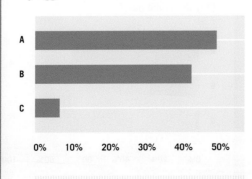

KEY

A No one will be doing the difficult stories in the future
B The public's right to know will disappear
C Local news will just cover light fun stories

BY THE NUMBERS

Older people worry most about local news, new poll for Index shows

JOURNALISTS HAVE BEEN worrying about the decline of local news reporting and its impact for years, but whether the public are also worried is more complex.

However, an exclusive poll carried out by YouGov for Index on Censorship this year, shows some public disquiet – mainly among older people.

Forty per cent of British adults over the age of 65 think that the public know less about what is happening in areas where local newspapers have closed down, compared with 28% of 18 to 24-year-olds, according to the poll about attitudes to local news.

More men than women feel the public know less about what is happening in areas when newspapers have closed (36% compared with 30%) .

When looked at region by region, Londoners are the most likely to feel that the public know less about what is going on if a local newspaper has closed down, with 38% saying that had happened, compared with the areas least likely to worry (32% in both Scotland and the rest of southern England).

All numbers according to YouGov data drawn from a representative sample of 1,840 British adults polled on 21-22 February 2019

Meanwhile, 26% of over-65s say that local politicians have too much power where local newspapers have closed, compared with only 16% of 18 to 24-year-olds.

The age divide is striking, with only 6% of 18 to 24-year-olds saying that their local newspaper has fewer resources to cover news than it used to, compared with 21% of those over 65.

Some people are finding different ways to view news, with 34% saying that alternative news sources have emerged in areas where local newspapers have closed down.

INSIDE LOCAL NEWS

"People feel too small to be heard"

Columnist **Libby Purves** talks to **Rachael Jolley** about working-class stories not being reported any more and the effects on society

48(01): 40/41 | DOI: 10.1177/0306422019842094

WHAT STRIKES ME most is how close we were to the people on the patch, even when they were part of a national story," said Times columnist Libby Purves of her first job at BBC Radio Oxford.

She explains how during the strikes at car manufacturer British Leyland the story was reported on the national news but she and her colleagues knew the assembly-line workers because they were their listeners.

"If the reason for yet another walkout was, in their view, being unfairly reported, they'd ring – or indeed turn up – and tell us so," she said.

"In the drought of 1976, Thames Water carried on urging restrictions in our area well after the rain started to fall and the reservoirs filled, and we could argue the case for people who had rung in who were obediently still rationing baths and using vegetable water to wash the

RIGHT: Local newspapers used to be a good way of finding out what the police are investigating

dog when there was no longer any need.

"My husband was up at Radio Humberside during the Cod War, and while ministers dominated the BBC Radio 4 Today programme, he was talking to skippers' wives, not as a brief 'colour' vox pop, but in a proper, long argument and discussion. Talking with him, and other ex-local journalists, what comes out strongly is that the old working class, of all generations, got a lot of airtime and were listened to in a way they have not been now for decades. Reflecting on the Brexit vote, that seems significant."

Purves, who has also been a presenter of BBC Radio 4's flagship political news programme Today, added: "The way news came in was different, too: court and council reporting – planning, housing, education, highways, finance – were the bread-and-butter of our

What comes out strongly is that the old working class, of all generations, got a lot of airtime and were listened to in a way they have not been now for decades

WHY SHOULD WE CARE ABOUT LOCAL JOURNALISM?

> " *A walk down many high streets would once have brought you into contact with the local newspaper office, where you could drop in and speak to a reporter or the editor. Other reporters would cover local court cases. Now, many of those offices have gone the same way as local travel agents or post offices. To find the shrunken staffs that once sat in them, you often need to look to out-of-town "hubs" where reporters covering a range of areas work together. In some cases, the newspapers can be physically situated 20 or 30 miles from the towns they purport to represent. People aren't stupid, they know this, and are aware a bond has been lost.*

STEPHEN KHAN, editor of The Conversation UK, worked as a journalist on the Kilmarnock Standard, Scotland "

newsroom, and in local government nobody seemed to have heard of PR or modern curating of news. You got right to the councillor or mayor responsible, whether it was a new shopping centre or a row over the fire service.

"In court reporting, the trust which locals put in known voices meant facts emerged which would be less likely to be confided [to] a national.

"Above all, reporters (and we feature-makers) spent a lot of time out and about – in my case, on an appalling moped.

"Nobody was enslaved to updating an on-line feed and, as it was radio, if a press release came in it didn't just get rewritten – a voice had to be found to explain and justify it."

A decline in local reporting, she feels, means "people feel less able to be in the conversation, raise their argument in proper detail: in other words, to count. Brexit is relevant here, I suspect.

"If local media haven't enough resources to drill down and investigate in detail the possible local effect of some big national policy change or event, communities don't have a chance to muster their objections fast enough," she said. "People feel they're too small to be heard." ⊗

Rachael Jolley is the editor of Index

INSIDE LOCAL NEWS

Fighting for funding

Ex-local newspaper editor **Peter Sands** talks to fellow UK editors about cash problems and how newspapers are now full of stories other people want them to print

48(01): 42/44 I DOI: 10.1177/0306422019842095

WHEN I WAS editing a British regional daily newspaper, The Northern Echo, it wasn't unusual for advertisers to threaten to withdraw their "favours" because they were unhappy with something we had written. I once published photographs of a fight between an irate customer and a business owner, and the company pulled its advertising. The boycott lasted six weeks until it realised it had nowhere else to peddle its wares. I was working for the late Westminster Press, the owner of daily and weekly newspapers throughout the UK, and answered to an independent editorial director, so there was never any question that commercial interests would override press freedom.

It did strike me, even then, that it was a precarious arrangement. We relied on businesses and local authorities for our revenue, but I had reporters, and bosses, more than happy to bite the hand that fed them. If the arrangement was precarious 30 years ago, it now dangles over a cliff. Advertisers have other routes to market, and classified, situations vacant, property and auto ads – once the source of millions of pounds – have all but dried up.

With declined revenue it is inevitable that staffing and the number and coverage of stories – particularly those that require some journalistic legwork – has also declined.

So how is journalism to be paid for? Is the advertising model on which the industry was built broken? Maybe not yet but, as Neil Benson, former editorial director of Trinity Mirror Regionals and now a media consultant, says, "it has sustained life-changing injuries". Alan Geere, who has edited titles around the globe, said: "I don't think the model is broken, it's just moved away from traditional print display and classified. Organisations and businesses still need to get their message out there. It's up to us to find the appropriate medium."

One area under pressure is the relationship newspapers have with councils. Local authorities are legally required to place public notices in newspapers – a guaranteed source of income – but some councils argue that is archaic. Others have their own publications, "Town Hall Pravdas", to put their own spin on council affairs and compete for revenue.

While editing the Hexham Courant, Colin Tapping saw evidence that councils begrudged having to place notices in newspapers they did not see eye-to eye with.

On one occasion, Tapping discovered notices from the Northumberland County Council were to be published in another paper, the Northumberland Gazette. He said: "I informed the council it was breaching its statutory obligations. The Courant enjoys one of the highest readership penetrations in the UK [and] the Northumberland Gazette has an official penetration of 0% in the Courant's circulation area.

"Investigations revealed the ban was ordered because the council was miffed by the Courant's coverage of changes to the charging structure at leisure centres. It was clear the

Paywalls are not effective locally, crowdfunding is limited and government funding brings independence questions

decision was to punish the Courant financially for its reporting. It amounted to censorship."

Mike Sassi, editor of the Nottingham Post, is witnessing a shift back to covering more council stories.

It follows the creation of 150 journalism jobs by the Local Democracy Reporting Service, with reporters funded by the BBC but working for regional news organisations. Its aim is to help fill a gap in the reporting of local democracy issues.

Sassi explained: "Our local democracy reporter, Kit Sandeman, has started to go to council meetings that had been dropped. He works through agendas, builds old-style relationships with politicians and turns up stories that may never have come to light. One was a decision to hold discussions about a controversial reorganisation of district and borough councils – affecting bin collections, school teaching, public parks and road building – behind closed doors.

"Our experience of the council is that it's usually a well-run, transparent organisation. However, a handful of politicians – perhaps politicians who had become unused to answering journalists' questions – decided they were going to have some of their discussions in private. And no one was going to stop them."

The bottom line is that journalism needs to find revenue that won't impinge on its independence. The search for digital revenue is immensely challenging, paywalls are not effective locally, crowdfunding is limited and funding by government brings independence questions. And until that revenue is found, campaigning and investigative journalism – with some notable exceptions – is struggling to survive. That is exacerbated by the fact that many newspapers now need to grow their digital audience to make money – and when skateboarding cats deliver a bigger audience than a six-week investigation into town hall jiggery-pokery, can editors justify time for serious spadework?

Allan Prosser, editor of the Irish Examiner, has concerns.

"Council and court reporting, which often provides the ammunition for investigative →

WHY SHOULD WE CARE ABOUT LOCAL JOURNALISM?

Ethically, we have to commit ourselves to truth and then, practically, we have to – and this sounds very simple but I'm going to say it at every possible venue – we have to subscribe or buy newspapers. We have to subscribe and buy paid-for media who actually hire investigative reporters because investigative reporters are the human link between our daily lives and the thing that we call media. There is nothing else. There's this immense internet with its almost infinite so-called information and then there are us human beings, but the only links really are the human beings whose jobs are to figure things out, and the only way for them to figure things out is for us to subscribe to newspapers. The idea that we should be getting our news for free makes much less sense than getting our auto repairs for free … If everyone picked up a newspaper on the way to work or we all subscribed to things we know are important, we would be in much better shape. The policy thing is that government – whether it is the EU or the United States or individual states – has to create the conditions where local media can flourish.

TIM SNYDER, a US historian and the author of The Road to Unfreedom, and On Tyranny

It was clear the decision was to punish the Courant financially for its reporting. It amounted to censorship

→ reporting, has declined and this is often made worse by opaque and disconnected information systems in local government and legal processes which obstruct rather than aid data journalism and scrutiny by reporters," he said.

"A less informed society where news is replaced by public relations, reactive commentary and agenda management by corporations and governments will become dangerously volatile and open to manipulation by special interests. Journalism is always imperfect but, as we have seen in the past decade, some of the alternatives threaten to be worse."

Geere added: "The squeeze on staff numbers and the increasing reliance on technology has led to journalists in many newsrooms confined to 'indoors play'. The result is that the community is not observed, let alone scrutinised, newspapers and their websites are full of 'news other people want you to print' and thousands of real people stories go untold."

Meanwhile Benson said: "Obviously, the most extreme examples of coverage disappearing are where loss-making titles have been closed down and, in some cases, communities have been left without a traditional source of local news. The 1,000 or so local titles that continue to publish are long past the point where any potential gap in coverage could be filled by asking the remaining reporters to simply work a bit harder to produce more stories. Nowadays, editors have to make choices about what to cover."

An editor of daily titles who does not want to be named believes there is still value in quality print journalism, particularly for the over-50s, but said: "Unfortunately, I don't think that can easily happen within the financial strictures of the big groups. Maybe we have to wait for the total break-up of the current newspaper industry and the re-emergence of locally owned, modestly profitable titles."

Hyperlocal titles may be one way forward but, as it stands, they are not the answer. Most are one-person operations that can't cover the courts, tackle the wrong-doers or have the deep pockets needed to defend legal threats. Those living in the community they are writing about are also probably less likely to rock the boat.

The route ahead is unclear. One editor said: "I'm uncomfortable with any kind of institutional funding, from the BBC, government or the digital beasts. Sooner or later that will mean a loss of independence. I think we have to accept that digital revenues will never replace print revenues, and that the old-fashioned newspaper model is doomed."

But Benson hits a more positive note. "There have been some encouraging signs that Google and Facebook recognise they will have to pay for the privilege of using that content. But while the £6m Facebook has pledged recently to support publishers in the UK is welcome, it is nowhere near adequate. An appropriate, sustainable levy to help publishers would be a start." He hopes that some of the ideas in the Cairncross Review [a UK government review into the sustainability, production and distribution of high-quality journalism in these times of change] will produce some workable solutions. Government subsidy, however, must surely be a no-no from the point of view of an independent press, he added.

The last word goes to Prosser, who believes journalism will need a diverse range of sources of funds and backers. But that, he says, "is a thesis, not an article". ⊗

Peter Sands *is the former editor of UK regional daily newspaper The Northern Echo*

`INSIDE LOCAL NEWS`

Staying alive

Local journalism is much needed in Italy but, as
Laura Silvia Battaglia reports, just doing your
job can be dangerous

48(01): 45/45 I DOI: 10.1177/0306422019842096

SANDRO RUOTOLO IS a veteran investigative reporter famous for the many years he
spent investigating the Mafia and Camorra in
southern Italy, initially for local news organisations and then on national television.

He says financial survival is not just an issue
for local news publications – it goes hand in
hand with concerns for their staff.

Now working in Naples for Fanpage, a web-
based TV channel with nine million followers,
he says local newspapers that have succeeded
in making the "life-saving transition to digital"
must innovate and adapt while also avoiding
a problem which although present at national
level, is felt more keenly locally: the conflict of
interest between editorial leadership and financial ownership.

He told Index: "When journalists, especially
local ones, probe such conflation of interests
because they believe in independent journalism,
they put themselves at
risk - physically at risk.

"The fact that there
are still 21 journalists,
20 working locally,
with police escorts be-
cause of death threats
received, is the fault of
all the other journalists
who are too closely
connected with politi-
cians and cultivate such
conflicts of interest."

Ruotolo, who has
received multiple
threats, was assigned a police escort. This was
revoked by interior minister Matteo Salvini,
then reinstated. The removal of his security was
criticised by the public which, says Ruotolo,
underlines the appetite for proper reporting.

"My experience proves the Italian people's
demand for information," he said. "In an age
of ignorance, the public is reclaiming its right
to hear the truth. To me, this is of enormous
political significance." ⊗

Translation by **Denise Muir**

Laura Silvia Battaglia *is a contributing
editor at Index*

WHY SHOULD WE CARE ABOUT LOCAL JOURNALISM?

"

*Local reporting in France and Belgium has often lacked audacity in holding local officials, companies or
institutions to account, or in covering potentially divisive stories. However, it has been providing an essential
public interest service by informing on concrete issues, by helping create a public forum and by giving a
visibility to many people and communities who were – or felt – shunned by national media. The demise
of local reporting undermines all journalism, creating black holes at the moment when understanding the
"backcountry" is crucial. It threatens to play the game of populism by exacerbating the sense of being
"dumped" and forgotten, of living in "fly-over/drive-by" towns and villages.*

JEAN-PAUL MARTHOZ, a Belgian journalist and columnist for Le Soir

"

INSIDE LOCAL NEWS

Public interest news is suffering

Former UK Culture Secretary **John Whittingdale** says not reporting on the activities of public institutions puts democracy at risk

48(01): 46/47 | DOI: 10.1177/0306422019842097

WHEN I WAS first elected to parliament in 1992 to represent Maldon, in the east of England, the district had two local newspapers. Both continue today but they bear little resemblance to the publications of 25 years ago. Then, one had an office in the high street where there was an editor, a deputy editor, reporters and photographers. The other, in neighbouring Chelmsford, had a full staff including a local government editor whose sole job was to cover the proceedings of the local councils.

Today, both papers have moved their offices far from the district. The main local paper is now 15 miles away and has an editor even further away who is responsible for all the papers covering the whole region. Its two reporters do their best but have only recently graduated from journalism college. It appears that there is virtually no fact-checking going on. Most photographs that appear are supplied to the paper rather than taken by a staff photographer. Often, articles appear to be simple reproductions of press releases in what Nick Davies of The Guardian calls "churnalism".

We are lucky in my part of Essex that at least two weekly newspapers still exist. Hundreds of local newspapers have closed around Britain in recent years. We have seen the loss of more than 200 titles and 6,000 frontline journalists in the past 12 years. All too often, it is "public interest news" – investigative journalism and the reporting of public institutions – that has suffered.

The decline in the reporting of local councils and other public institutions represents a threat to democracy. With central government devolving powers to locally elected mayors, councils and police commissioners, electors are not able to find accurate information about their policies and performance, in order to decide how to vote.

The situation is mirrored in the courts. The principle that justice should not only be done but also be seen to be done is undermined if court proceedings go unreported. Research by the University of the West of England found that of 220 cases heard in one week in a Bristol court, a reporter attended just three of them.

The British government recognised the serious consequences of the decline of local media in its recently published review, A Sustainable Future for Journalism, conducted by Dame Frances Cairncross. Her report makes some useful recommendations, including a new institute for public interest news, and tax relief to support public interest journalism. The government is now considering her findings.

As Secretary of State for Culture, Media

ONLINE ONLY MEANS NO NEWS FOR THE ELDERLY

ROBERT HALFON, THE member of parliament for Harlow, in Essex, UK, recently said he was being contacted by elderly citizens who could no longer find out about local news as the local papers had closed down. They were ringing his office to find out what was happening in their areas.

He told the BBC that local news websites were all very well, but "you have to be online to look at it".

He said not everyone had access to online news, adding: "It's not just older people, because there are a lot of people who don't have access to a computer or the internet. They may have a phone but they can't afford the data package or they might only look at it now and then."

Electors are not able to find accurate information about their policies and performance

and Sport in 2016, I worked with the BBC to set up the local democracy reporting scheme. Under this initiative, the BBC has provided £8 million for each of the next nine years to fund the employment of more than 150 journalists in partnership with local news providers. These journalists provide factual reports of what is going on in local councils and other public bodies. These are made available to the BBC and shared with more than 700 other media organisations. Already some 54,000 stories have been filed. Although it is small, it is making a difference and the scheme could easily be expanded to cover the proceedings of more elected bodies and courts.

The scheme is already attracting interest from other countries. The most obvious source of funds to expand it are online technology companies such as Google and Facebook, who are now the biggest distributors of news content. Neither employs journalists; instead they distribute stories gathered by the traditional media. It is strongly in their interests to support such schemes (see p44) as without professional journalists there will be no reliable news stories. If these companies would invest just a small proportion of their profits in this initiative, they could help sustain local journalism rather than destroy it – and, in doing so, bolster local democracy and the justice system.

We have all relied on our local newspapers over the years, and my fear is that only when they are gone will we realise their vital importance to democratic society. ⊗

__John Whittingdale__ is the member of parliament for Maldon, Essex, UK

WHY SHOULD WE CARE ABOUT LOCAL JOURNALISM?

I'd say the state of local news in Nigeria is gradually gaining momentum again as a result of the emerging new media platforms, mainly on the internet. But, before, it was in decline. Conversations were driven by agendas put out by international media narratives and the national and political agenda, ignoring the very people whose stories needed to be told. But with the reach and access to internet connectivity in Nigeria and the new frontier of internet-based news organisations, the situation is changing. However, local or community newspapers that help to report stories from rural communities have declined. As a matter of fact, I can say that has led to the death of local news from these sources in Nigeria as most community newspapers or community radio no longer function across the country.

MERCY ABANG, a journalist with NewsWireNGR based in Abuja, Nigeria

Readers are no longer reading what they should know, but are fed with what they are expected to enjoy

→ Today the most popular news app in China belongs not to a news company but to a tech company called Jinri Toutiao. It relies on an algorithm to figure out what people like. Readers are no longer reading what they should know, but are fed with what they are expected to enjoy.

Independent publishing channels, or "self-media" – the most popular being the platform provided by Wechat's "public account" function, which works a little like Facebook's public pages – are also picking up advertising and readers. Most of the media are driven by clicks. Even the media that care about social issues have to be careful to not touch sensitive topics, as they don't have permission from the government for that sort of reporting.

It has been difficult for the new media to take over the social responsibilities from the dying traditional local newspapers.

"The fact that the traditional local newspapers belonged to the party and the government gave them limitations, but at the same time also a kind of protection. The media run by [others] could be shut down so easily," said Fang, the former Southern Weekly journalist.

Meanwhile, charges of "illegal reporting" and defamation can be used easily on private media owners. One incident happened in the spring of 2018 when a doctor was detained without charge for three months after describing a traditional Chinese medicine wine as "poison" in his Wechat blog – offending the manufacturer, which had a close relationship with the government.

But despite that, Chuchu is not entirely pessimistic. She remains hopeful about the internet, as it provides accessibility for more people to have their voices heard.

"Journalists used to be the only people who were out there revealing the problem – the only ones who determined what was worth being reported and what was not. The internet makes it easy for everybody to speak out and be the supervisors," she said.

However, Chuchu's hopes might not be realised. Every time I visit my uncle in a northern Chinese village, he and his friends make tons of complaints to me about what is happening: the corrupt village chief, the pollution from the paper factory, and the way in which village land is being sold. But there isn't a local newspaper, and the only "journalists" are a few young women working for the government-controlled TV station, which only announces the officials' decisions and praises how well the government is doing. It is the same in all of China's small towns and villages.

I have asked them why they don't write about their concerns on the internet, but none of these old people know how to use the internet properly, and they are worried that government or party loyalists would take revenge.

And that leaves them with the little power to challenge the authorities, and that is probably how the authorities would like it. ⊗

Karoline Kan is a journalist and Beijing editor at chinadialogue. Her book, Under Red Skies, Three Generations of Love, Loss, and Hope in China, was published in March

India shifts local

Ahead of India's elections, **Rituparna Chatterjee** finds local journalists battling to get paid and do their jobs

48(01): 51/53 | DOI: 10.1177/0306422019842099

DEMAND FOR LOCAL news is rising in India, and with the national elections coming up in April and May, how accurately the news – particularly local news – is reported will be vital for communities all over this vast country.

An appetite for information, combined with a digital media boom piggybacking on cheap data connectivity, has enabled the mushrooming of regional news outfits catering to a new audience hooked on their smartphones.

Some 620 million people are forecast to be online in India in 2019. And while newspapers struggle to stay afloat elsewhere in the world, India registered a growth in the number of print publications during 2016-17.

Soaring literacy rates have also helped this growth – and if it is compelling, local news in India has a huge audience. "The interesting micro-stories of small groups of people written with a larger, national perspective always do well," said Sunetra Choudhury, political editor at New Delhi-based news broadcaster NDTV.

She cites a story about the reminiscences of the bodyguard of Mayawati, head of the Bahujan Samaj Party and a prominent politician from India's lower-caste communities. The report, which had immense regional appeal, was recently the most popular for the broadcaster.

In the south of India there is also a constant demand for, and supply of, local news. And Sneha Koshy, who heads NDTV in Kerala, says this is vital for holding politicians to account.

She describes how news outlets have influenced politics in the state's Kollam district. A story about illegal mining was highlighted initially by protestors but was picked up by local news and a few national channels. It became a very important regional story, enabled by digital storytelling which forced local authorities, including politicians, to respond.

"When people who know what their rights are raise an issue through local news, MPs know they will have to answer for it during elections," Koshy said.

One issue is that news from broadcasters such as NDTV jostles for attention with "fake news" on social media sites.

Facebook in India, under pressure from the government, has recently expanded its fact-checking network to help stop the spread of misinformation.

Dheerendra Gupta, a crime reporter with the Patrika daily in Satna, in the central Indian state of Madhya Pradesh, has a nickname for administrators of social media groups that spread "fake news".

"These 'Whatsapp Journalists' are a menace. They undermine the hard work we put into fact checking," he said.

Whatsapp groups can highlight real problems, such as the illegal mining in Kollam, but they are also vulnerable to being flooded with "fake news" and political propaganda. This has become a worrying trend in a country where vulnerable communities live in close quarters and rumours can spark violence.

"There's huge demand for local news ahead of the polls. But misinformation on Whatsapp groups run by people who are not →

When people who know what their rights are, raise an issue through local news MPs know they will have to answer for it during elections

→ journalists has the potential to cause a lot of harm," Gupta said.

Another problem for accurate local news reporting can be journalists themselves.

India's rural journalists tell a story of deprivation and of living in the shadow of threats. Amit Singh, a special correspondent for a local daily in Satna, in the central Indian state of Madhya Pradesh, now regrets taking up journalism as a career choice. But this wasn't always the case. Singh, who is also a stringer for Hindustan Times, takes great pride in telling the stories he has covered in Satna which has a population of about 300,000. His voice perks up with relish in narrating his encounters with *dacoits* – bandits – operating in remote terrains of the state.

"I've written about the nexus of *dacoits* and politicians. I've written about a woman *dacoit* whose whereabouts even the police did not know. I'm the first to reach a spot, often even before the police," he told Index.

"But for the past few years, I have been ruing my decision. There's no money. Not enough to survive. It's a daily battle." Singh says his newspaper, the daily Star Samachar, pays him such a small salary that he relies on other means to supplement his income.

"But I am better off than most small-town reporters. I have land in the village nearby where my family lives and I only pay for electricity and rent in Satna. My food comes from the fields," says Singh, who comes from a family of farmers. Singh says politicians and police are keen to censor news and put pressure on local reporters. He once turned down a bribe of the equivalent of $7,000 because his conscience wouldn't allow him.

"Stringers are powerful sources of local news. If they are paid a decent salary, this racket

of blackmailing will clean up," he said.

Mahtab Alam, executive editor of website The Wire Urdu, says news in sensitive areas can get diluted if stringers either do not want to jeopardise their personal safety by reporting it, or become morally compromised. Journalists in India have been killed after investigating controversial stories or challenging local politicians.

One of the reasons for the reliance on stringers is that news organisations have struggled financially. Hundreds of small news operations in India's small towns and cities were badly hit by a move by the federal government in 2016 to ban high-value banknotes, ostensibly to crack down on corruption.

Small businesses that typically fund local news outlets are dependent on cash, and so stopped advertising. News outlets responded by firing reporters and outsourcing news gathering to a network of poorly-paid freelancers.

Singh says most small newspapers have learnt to back a few selected local politicians rather than a political party. Smaller newspapers sometimes lift unverified content from the internet because it saves money.

Shams Ur Rehman Alavi, a journalist from Bhopal, the capital city of Madhya Pradesh, says there's a dire need for micro-local news. Multi-edition Hindi newspapers with huge circulations, such as Dainik Bhaskar and Dainik Jagran, bring in their own selective news culture, which often ignores local issues. "Take, for example, tribal areas of MP," he said. "Even if a district has a population of four million, there's no news coverage from there. Media houses focus on state and national news. Local news gets suppressed. And there's a complete 'othering' of tribals and indigenous people."

There's also pressure to follow news from Twitter and Whatsapp, a world alien to many small-town journalists in their late 40s and 50s who struggle to make sense of the newsy internet culture, says Pankaj Shukla, the resident editor of Subah Savere, a newspaper based in Bhopal and Indore.

We are not changemakers at this point, we are in crisis.... The space for serious journalism is shrinking

CREDIT: Shailesh Andrade/Reuters

"We are not changemakers at this point, we are in crisis…. The space for serious journalism is shrinking," he said.

He identifies two problems plaguing local news operations: social media such as Whatsapp as a news source and in-house infrastructure problems or, as he wryly states in Hindi, "*paisa nahi hai* (there's no money)".

Patricia Mukhim, editor of Shillong Times, the oldest English language newspaper in the north-east Indian state of Meghalaya, echoes Shukla's words. "If we think we are influencers in some way, it's a mirage. In the end, all that matters is money," she said.

But all is not bleak. Journalist Neelesh Mishra founder of one of India's biggest rural media platforms, Gaon Connection, says that in today's news environment, his organisation is a global case study of how an independent local media can thrive without paid news, corporate or political influence, and with no ad revenue.

Gaon Connection was among 10 media outlets in India selected for funding from YouTube as part of the Google News Initiative. Where some local news outlets have failed, Mishra says he has found new revenue streams from the content his platform produces.

"Even the office driver and the office boy have been trained to be content creators. Writing a story is a craft few have, but creating relevant video content is possible by anyone who has a smartphone," Mishra said. He aims to create a large enough network so that it becomes a powerful voice for people in rural India.

As India goes to the polls starting in April this year, it is not the big media but a trusty network of local reporters, with their ears to the ground, that most Indians will rely on. ⊗

Rituparna Chatterjee is an independent journalist based in New Delhi, India

Remote controller

Viktor Orbán's Hungarian government and friends now oversee all significant local media and, as **Dan Nolan** reports, sometimes they are all repeating the same stories

48(01): 54/56 | DOI: 10.1177/0306422019842100

IT IS IN the provinces where Hungarian elections are won and lost. That is why, in the run-up to the European elections, the Hungarian government has made sure that its control of the local press is as tight as possible.

Over the past nine years, the right-wing government of Viktor Orbán has taken over the country's media with the impunity that only a super-majority allows.

The most widely reported closure has been the country's de facto newspaper of record, Népszabadság, in Budapest. But it is the takeover of local papers in provincial towns, where lots of people get their news, that is the most pernicious.

A visit to a newsagent's shop outside the capital soon illustrates how strictly regional newspapers now toe the government line

BELOW: Montage of the webpages of Hungary's regional press showing they all carry the same story

– most notably Orbán's highly successful anti-immigration rhetoric. The papers run headlines such as "Migration pressure growing in the region", years after the migration wave through Hungary ended, and emigration became the main challenge for the economy.

Meanwhile, the government is consistently portrayed as successfully managing the ongoing funding crises in Hungary's health and education sectors, with headlines that emphasise promised spending hikes and pay rises.

Regional newspapers also avoid stories embarrassing to Orbán, such as the European Anti-Fraud Office last year uncovering serious irregularities in an EU tender won by a company partially owned by his son-in-law.

Since 2017, 13 of Hungary's 18 provincial newspapers have been bought by Orbán's proxy, Lőrinc Mészáros; three by the controversial Austrian businessman Heinrich Pecina; and the remaining three by the late media mogul Andy Vajna.

In December 2018, the government took a further step in its dominance of the media. Claiming the protection of conservative media to be of "national strategic importance", the Orbán regime made all local papers the property of the Central European Press and Media Foundation (Kesma).

The government decree allowed Kesma to swallow up 476 outlets. It was issued at short notice and sidestepped the usual legal requirements of media and competition law. In one go, the decree created one of Europe's largest media holdings, in a country with fewer than ten million people.

"All regional dailies belong to the Fidesz media conglomerate now," said Gábor Polyák, head of Hungary's leading independent media monitor, Mérték. "It is not about business, it is pure politics."

Although the number of subscribers to local newspapers has declined significantly in recent years, 400,000 copies are sold every day, which means about 1.5 million readers, according to Mérték.

"It is clear that the national news [articles] are edited centrally [and] articles are taken from government outlets," said Polyák. "The bias is very clear: in the local news there are no real politics, they spread the political content of Magyar Idők and other Fidesz outlets. Experts in articles are from [state outlets] Echo TV and M1. The bias is very clear."

The new system "clearly evokes communist times", Zselyke Csaky, Freedom House research director for Europe and Eurasia, told Index. "The centralisation sends a message that the private media sector property supporting government goals was never really private property. It's also a reminder to loyal oligarchs and businessmen close to the ruling party that they are tools, useful only insofar as their interests overlap with the government interest of the day."

Index spoke to a journalist and former long-term employee at Délmagyarország, Hungary's biggest regional paper, which covers the Csongrád area from Szeged, the country's third largest town. It serves as an example of how the government has operated to discredit and shut down regional papers.

"Around a decade ago, another news website named Szegedma (Szeged Today) appeared in the city. Szegedma worked as a mouthpiece for Fidesz party delegates," said the journalist, who spoke on condition of anonymity.

It published a letter which it claimed had been sent by a socialist party MP to Szeged mayor László Botka, telling him to wait until after the April 2018 elections before settling migrants in Szeged. The letter, which the website claimed to have received from a reader, turned out to be fake.

Pressure was also brought to bear on the Délmagyarország editorial desk, claimed the journalist. János Lázár, a Fidesz minister and the erstwhile mayor of Csongrad's other city, Hódmezővásárhely, was in regular contact.

"There were several occasions when Lázár called editors to spike articles – he would tell the editor that they would cancel all subscriptions if we wrote a story," said the journalist.

Once the takeover of Délmagyarország was complete, former Fidesz councillor Gábor Bonifert, who edited the rival news website,

The local and rural press is very important in Hungary because propaganda is successful if there is no alternative

was installed as editor-in-chief and all but two of the staff quit or were fired.

Opponents to Orbán's media takeover include NGOs and independent journalists.

Dalma Dojcsák, a lawyer who leads the political freedoms project at the Hungarian Civil Liberties Union (TASZ), is suing the government on grounds of fair competition.

"We knew that we wanted to do something with this problem that has a significant effect on the media market in Hungary and people's right to access free and non-biased media outlets in Hungary," she said. But, she needed a partner who could help.

TASZ contacted Szabad Pécs (Free Pécs), an online outlet established in 2017 by two journalists. Szabad Pécs co-founder Attila Babos told Index: "The lawsuit was TASZ's idea, as it needed a partner in the litigation who was involved in the media market. I immediately said yes."

In 15 years as a local journalist, Babos has witnessed the collapse of independent local media. "From 2004 to 2016 I worked at →

MEDIA RESTRICTIONS BY NUMBERS

||||||||||||||||||||||||||||||||||||||||||||||||||||||

Index's project Mapping Media Freedom tracked violations in Hungary

218 INCIDENTS OF media freedom violations were reported in Hungary from May 2014 to 31 July 2018, including:
- 36 reports of intimidation of journalists
- 41 reports of legislation or court orders restricting media freedom
- 55 reports of preventing reporting through various obstacles
- 32 reports of public ridicule of a media professional

Source: Mapping Media Freedom

ABOVE: A protester holds a copy of Népszabadság newspaper aloft during an anti-government demonstration in 2016. The paper had been closed down just weeks before

→ the local daily newspaper Dunántúli Napló, the local daily of Baranya county," he said. "It used to be very professional, highly appreciated and financially very successful, even after the financial crisis of 2008.

"However, the relentless media domination strategy of Fidesz saw the net close in on independent journalism in Pécs. Due to pressure from authorities, Axel Springer had to sell Dunántúli Napló (and many other newspapers) to a Fidesz-linked company," he said.

After the deal, Babos and several colleagues left the company, knowing that they would be pressured to follow orders that "overwrite the ethics and best practices of professional journalism in favour of the political agenda".

Anticipating his dismissal, Babos started planning to launch a new independent local news site, choosing the name Szabad Pécs to echo the Radio Free Europe service that served Hungary during the communist era.

"It was founded in March 2017 as a Facebook page, but within three weeks launched its own domain," Babos said. "The goal is to become the voice of the region and to report about local news that is nobody else reporting. This work is not easy, but not many advertisers appear because they are afraid, so the situation has deteriorated. The local and rural press is very important in Hungary because propaganda is successful if there is no alternative." ⊗

Dan Nolan is a freelance journalist based in Budapest

Rocky times

Monica O'Shea, who worked as a regional journalist for five years, worries that remote communities in Australia are losing their local news

48(01): 57/59 | DOI: 10.1177/0306422019842101

GEOFF VIVIAN, A regional journalist in Geraldton, Western Australia, worries about areas of his vast country which are now without a newspaper.

"They will never have a local newspaper again," he said, adding that he believes the best they can expect is an A4 local newsletter.

Vivian, who has worked for Seven West media for four years and as a freelance reporter in local areas for a further 10, says that while a keen young local journalist may feel that reporting on councils in rural communities is an amazing opportunity to dig out stories, he believes many experienced journalists would rather work in a city.

"Many people see local government as small potatoes and don't want to cover it," he said. "The problem is it is the tier of government that is closest to our lives that is paid the least attention."

There is increased concern about the future of local news in Australia. Regional newspapers are closing, television stations are broadcasting more centrally, and the recent merger of major media corporations Fairfax and Nine is likely to mean more titles closing.

Despite this, newspapers are still a relatively popular way for people to get the news. According to the Sydney Morning Herald, they are read by 67% of Australians, with 10 million people reading metropolitan newspapers and 6.3 million people reading regional and community titles.

Over the years, local news outlets have been responsible for exposing some of the biggest corruption scandals in Australia's history. Eleven years ago, the government sacked Wollongong council in New South Wales following the Illawarra Mercury's extensive coverage of corruption, including allegations of developers bribing staff.

In a similar example of local journalists breaking news, Newcastle Herald reporter Joanne McCarthy wrote 350 articles exposing the sexual abuse of children, primarily by Catholic clergy, in the Hunter Valley.

Her coverage was so damning that a Royal Commission was established to investigate, and McCarthy won a Gold Walkley Award, an honour for excellence in journalism, in 2013.

Former Prime Minister Julia Gillard, in what she described as her "very final moments" in the top job, thanked the journalist for her "remarkable struggle to tell the story".

These are shining examples of how regional reporters can break the news that matters in local communities, but without local newspapers keeping a watching brief, any corruption or scandals in the future may remain unreported in communities.

The number of newspaper closures makes grim reading and smaller community papers have closed recently across the nation, despite being owned by major media players News Corp, Seven West and Fairfax Media.

In November 2017, Fairfax closed six western Sydney titles, reducing its suburban mastheads from 16 to 10. This resulted in the loss of 11 jobs.

Similarly, Community News Group, owned by News Corp and Western Australian newspapers, shut five papers in August 2018.

Fairfax Regional Newspapers closed the Wagin Argus, the Merredin-Wheatbelt Mercury and the Central Midlands and Coastal Advocate in regional Western Australia in 2015. →

The problem is it is the tier of government that is closest to our lives that is paid the least attention

→ The impact of the Fairfax and Nine merger on regional media in Australia is yet to be seen. With Fairfax owning 160 titles, all eyes are on what the result of this partnership will be for local papers.

When speaking to investors, the chief executive of Nine News Hugh Marks stated that regional newspapers would do better in "some other environment".

Local TV is also in decline. Regional TV stations have an obligation to broadcast a certain level of local content every year, but many are not meeting their target.

The Australian Communications and Media Authority report, Local Content in Regional Australia 2017, analysed local television coverage in 11 areas of South Australia, Western Australia, Northern Territory, Victoria, New South Wales, Queensland and Tasmania.

Research found many of these towns were ending television bulletins, reducing local content or collaborating with newspaper journalists to fulfil their local content requirements.

Brenton Vanstone, deputy chairman of Regional Development Australia Yorke and Mid North (an organisation which aims to boost economic growth in this area of South Australia), and former mayor of the city of Port Pirie – a city 223km north of Adelaide – says he misses local news on television.

"When you turn on the television, all our news is from interstate," he told Index. "Local news is now read from Canberra and it used to be read in Port Pirie."

He also talks fondly about local programmes – including Women's World and Panel Probe – that used to be made locally but which are no longer broadcast.

BELOW: A cattle farmer reads a newspaper in rural Australia. There is increasing concern for the future of newspapers in regional areas

CREDIT: Andrew McInnes/Alamy

Staff cuts, newspaper closures and fewer reporters on the ground raise an important question about government accountability in regional areas and local towns.

Despite many rural areas still having a local newspaper, the quality of coverage and ability to cover council meetings is declining, and Vanstone says the original purpose of newspapers is now not being met.

Fairfax Regional Media cut back the Port Pirie Recorder to one edition a week in 2012 and made further staff cuts in 2015.

Like many of South Australia's regional papers owned by the company, the publication has focused on growing its digital readership in recent years.

"That small country paper you once had is no longer viable," said Vanstone, adding that the harsh reality is that proprietors need to make a profit, and if a paper doesn't pay, its days are numbered.

He also believes local newspapers are heavily influenced by their dependence on advertising revenue from councils and local businesses in regional towns, so they are unlikely to be critical for fear of losing revenue.

Andrew Jeffries, a Parramatta councillor in Sydney, says community newspapers often have only one journalist across two or three mastheads. He believes this is not a broad enough approach and could lead to slanted coverage.

In Western Australia, Vivian believes that the success of local newspapers lies with the fact that they have journalists who are familiar with the people and the country.

"A steady stream of new faces with no contacts and no appreciation of local issues means stories that the locals will pick holes in because they lack context," he said. "Journos who know the people and the district tend not to stay around unless they become the editor."

He said that at Geraldton Newspapers, based 425km north of Perth, the number of reporters has recently been cut and independent news outlets are also suffering.

Articles from local churches and heritage societies are unlikely to win investigative journalism awards or expose corruption in local government

"In regional Western Australia, most newspapers are owned by one of two groups. Two thirds are owned by Seven West and one third are owned by Fairfax," he said.

While the journalists who remain are experienced, Vivian admits the job is tougher with fewer staff.

"Where I work, this time last year there were seven journalists – now there are five," he said.

Another regional journalist from South Australia, who wants to remain anonymous, says his publication is the poorer for cutting staff. "Councils are getting tougher to cover," he told Index. "The coverage in local areas has become more human interest-focused."

But there is some evidence that rural communities in Australia will continue producing community newsletters and independent newspapers if the major players disappear.

In the tiny town of Wandearah, 180km from Adelaide, the heritage society recently started producing its own local newsletter. Many other towns throughout Australia are doing the same.

But while these are enjoyable to read, articles from local churches and heritage societies are unlikely to win investigative journalism awards or expose corruption in local government.

There is no doubt that while human interest news has a future in rural communities, hard news reporting and the future of newspapers are at risk.

And when a paper goes, part of the community goes as well. ⊗

Monica O'Shea is a journalist who has worked for the Port Pirie Recorder and Flinders News in South Australia

Making local neighbourhoods great again

New business models based on technology and the involvement of readers are boosting journalism in Spain, writes **Silvia Nortes**

48(01): 60/61 | DOI: 10.1177/0306422019842102

DIGITAL OUTLETS AND new newspapers focusing on local news are challenging the Madrid nationals for readers. Many were set up by journalists who lost their jobs during the media shake-up of 2007 at the start of the financial crisis. At least three out of every 10 new media created in Spain from 2008 to 2014 had a regional and local scope, according to a study by the Universidad Autónoma de Barcelona.

These outlets are gaining importance and interest among readers, and implementing new technology and business models. The question is whether the outlets have the resources and clout to hold government and public agencies to account and carry out in-depth investigations.

Somos Malasaña, (We are Malasaña), is one of the most successful of this new breed of journalism. The first of its kind in Spain, set up in 2009 in one of Madrid's hippest areas, has a current average of 150,000 readers a month. "We believed that, even though local news in Madrid was being swallowed by national issues, there was an audience looking for hyperlocal information," editor Antonio Pérez told Index.

Somos's content is different from mainstream media and doesn't replicate agency news, said Pérez. Hyperlocals are considered by many to strengthen democracy featuring voices that don't normally appear in traditional media, such as neighbourhood associations. "Somos Malasaña became more than a newspaper: it is a virtual square," he explained.

The readers' involvement is the greatest value for the public, added Pérez, with the information collected having a lot to do with interacting with readers, as well. "We started by getting in touch with associations, cultural centres and businesses, as well as the city council. We became the best connoisseurs of what was going on. Now, authorities and mainstream media follow us as sources of information."

Despite this, hyperlocalism can lead stories considered difficult being left out due to the lack of human and financial resources. This can include in-depth investigations on big corruption cases or judicial processes.

"We may have fewer financial resources and, certainly, there is less chance that big issues of significance happen in our area, but it [does] happen sometimes," said Pérez.

The site concentrates on culture and useful information such as street repairs, the opening of new neighbourhood spaces and interviews with prominent figures from the district.

Many traditional newspapers, including nationals such El Mundo, are adapting by increasing their online presence. Spain, according to the Reuters Institute, has "some of the most diverse and competitive digital-born news brands in Europe".

The same is also happening locally. El Correo de Andalucía, a local media outlet, has tried to adapt to the new digital environment, but with less success. Founded in 1899, it was Spain's second oldest newspaper, focusing mainly on the city of Seville, publishing reports and interviews with local leaders and covering the neighbourhood. In 2018, it closed its print edition to become digital only because of financial problems.

The newspaper had been losing more than €100,000 ($113,000) every month for five years, the majority of the workers have been dismissed, and only a small number of pieces are bylined by staff. It depends heavily on agency news and press releases.

El Correo's staff are reluctant to speak about the situation and say it is too early to assess progress. But it is clear it is having an impact on the quality of the content.

Nonetheless, this might change in the future, because the company's president, Antonio Morera, is considering creating a "quality weekly for in-depth issues", while using the website for daily news.

Being small also makes local and hyperlocal journalism especially vulnerable to external influence because of its dependence on corporate and public sector advertising.

Advertising remains the main source of funding (81.5%) for digital media, although public funding is growing in importance.

Somos Malasaña became more than a newspaper: it is a virtual square

Media researcher Juan Manuel Moreno worries that "having a more direct contact with local companies, institutions and administrations, with fewer intermediaries", makes this type of media more susceptible to "receiving interference in their editorial line".

Thia isn't just a problem for local media, Pérez says. "No major newspaper has dared to publish information contrary to a big advertiser. Of course, there are local media that would not survive without subsidies, and many others that are immersed in local council press offices. In any case, the journalists' ethics should prevail."

Somos Malasaña does not receive any subsidy and most of its funds come from organising local events. Only a small amount of funds come from local advertisers, and sponsored information is accepted "only if the content is relevant to our audience and remains local". They say that projects such as Somos Malasaña annoy because they are uncontrollable – either by authorities or by companies.

In El Correo's case, changes in ownership influenced its funding. It was even accused of being controlled by the socialist party PSOE, which in 2013 invested €65,000 in institutional advertising. At present, the newspaper is supported by Morera and Vallejo Communication, the company of El Correo's president Antonio Morera. El Correo's staff refuse to make any statements on funding and advertising.

"Hyperlocal journalism will be a dominant trend during the next few years," Pérez concluded. Somos Malasaña and El Correo exemplify Spanish local media's efforts to make neighbourhood reporting great again. ⊗

Silvia Nortes is a freelance journalist, based in Murcia, Spain

OPPOSITE: A woman outside a bookshop in Malasaña, one of central Madrid's hippest areas

Banning controversial speech won't solve the issues

Kneejerk bans on anonymity, controversy and angry activism online won't make things better – they could actually make it harder to make things better, argues **Jodie Ginsberg**

48(01): 62/63 I DOI: 10.1177/0306422019842104

FACEBOOK TURNED 15 this year. I was in San Francisco for its birthday, seated in its vast new headquarters, surveying swathes of a valley that has been eaten up by tech giants. Looking out at the acres of office buildings, it was almost impossible to believe that a company of this size – a company that has nearly two billion active users, nearly a third of the world's population – is really still only a spotty teenager. So enormous have the Likes of Facebook become, so ubiquitous is the technology of social media, it's easy to forget just how recent this revolution is.

But we need to remember. If we don't, we risk rushing into fixes for the problems unleashed by this new technology that could have far more damaging consequences.

We've had just 15 years to adjust to social media. That's not even two decades to get accustomed to the idea that we can now publicise every thought, every feeling – not just to the people we know and love but to people we have never met and to groups and individuals who are perhaps thousands of miles away, or seated in positions of power. And all at the touch of a button.

This new ability to megaphone your every opinion has unleashed a wave of vile behaviour. It has given licence to every racist and bigot to pronounce their hateful views; it has allowed groups of people to form in order to taunt others they dislike; and it has created a culture in which dislike and offence have become performative – where individuals become ever more outrageous to garner attention (and funding).

It's easy to see why this has engendered a panicked "something must be done" response. Politicians, in particular, like nothing more than to be seen to be doing something. And while we may need new laws to deal with issues such as transparency of political advertising online, targeting problematic, but nevertheless legal, speech through the technology companies that have allowed this to happen should concern us.

It is true that social media companies have been slow to take responsibility for the ills unleashed on their platforms. Laying the blame exclusively at their doors – and proposing technical fixes and new forms of controls on online speech – risks undermining the hugely positive aspects of social media (and of freedom of speech more generally). It also forgets that we as a society have had so little time to adjust to this new form of communication; and it absolves individual users of any personal responsibility for their actions.

If we want to improve social media, we need to do two things. First, we need to step away from the notion that banning controversial speech will solve the issues. It won't, not least because it is almost impossible to agree on a definition that can be applied in

> *It's easy to see why this has engendered a panicked "something must be done" response*

such a way that only "bad speech" will be targeted.

Trans activists and radical feminists are discovering this as debates rage on social media about what constitutes hate speech in discussions about what we mean by the terms "man" and "woman".

Anti-racism campaigners have discovered this when their accounts have been suspended for trying to share the vile abuse they receive as evidence, as have the activists whose Facebook accounts were suspended in Burma for documenting genocide.

A newspaper in Norway discovered this when it tried to post an award-winning photo documenting the horrors of the Vietnam war and was caught out by a ban that outlawed naked photos.

Billions of pieces of content are posted online every day. The idea that we might be able to come up with a technical solution – or even an army of moderators – to effectively weed out all bad speech is nonsensical.

This is why the second solution is the most important. If we want to improve the quality of discussions on social media, we need to look in the mirror. Social media giants might be enabling us to spout hateful invective, and law enforcement might be ill-equipped to deal with actual illegal behaviour online, but the people ultimately responsible for the tone of discourse on social media are us. And – good news – we can use it how we want.

That means we can harness its power to engage communities of like-minded people for good, as Twitter activists did when seeking to protect a Saudi teenager who sought asylum in Thailand, or as #MeToo campaigners do when calling out sexual abuse. The point is that doing both (mobilising for evil and mobilising for good) rely on the same technology and often use the same language and behaviour:

a marshalling of supporters; the use of the language of anger, invective and challenge; the cloak of anonymity.

Instead of trying to tackle these characteristics as inherently negative, we need to see them as simultaneously necessary and problematic and learn to navigate these quirks rather than try to eliminate them.

After all, as is pointed out to Samuel Johnson in the TV comedy series Blackadder, all dictionaries since the first have been used to look up rude words. This isn't a reason to ban them.

Those growing up in a digital world are far more aware of this than those of us whose early communication tools were pen and paper, a telephone, a few TV channels and a bunch of analogue radio stations. This generation sees and understands the power of the internet, its power for good and the way it can be used for ill. They will be the people who shape new technologies and help tackle the power of internet giants. More importantly, they will work out how their own behaviour forms part of this new norm. ⊗

Jodie Ginsberg *is the Index CEO*

BELOW: A woman
lights a candle in
tribute to murdered
mayor Pawel Adamo-
wicz at the European
Solidarity Centre
in Gdansk, Poland,
January 2018

CREDIT: SOPA Imag... Limited/Alamy Stock Photo

IN FOCUS

Turning off the searchlights

Independent rescue boats have been forced out of the sea by government deals so it is now almost impossible to discover details of refugees trying to cross to Italy. **Alessio Perrone** reports

48(01): 66/67 I DOI: 10.1177/0306422019842103

WHEN THE RESCUE boat Aquarius was pulled from duty in December 2018, the Italian government celebrated on social media.

"UPDATE. The #Aquarius boat terminates its activity... This is good," tweeted Matteo Salvini, Italy's right-wing populist interior minister.

It was seen as a victory: the Aquarius's withdrawal was the final act of a campaign to remove all rescue boats run by non-governmental organisations from the central Mediterranean – the area between Libya, Malta and Italy.

But as well as carrying out rescues, these boats documented the numbers of deaths at sea, allowed journalists on board and reported human rights violations. Without them, external observers have disappeared, and many suspect that deaths and human rights violations now elude public scrutiny.

Nick Romaniuk, the search and rescue co-ordinator of the Aquarius, says the area has turned into an "information black hole", yet the overflowing boats of refugees are rarely out of the Italian media, and immigration is a subject at the heart of current political battles.

Tommaso Fusco, a junior editor at Open Migration, a website covering stories about migration, told Index: "Deaths at sea continue, and there are still very many, but they are much less talked about because there isn't a third party that records them – and when there is one, it is not always listened to."

Deaths are still recorded, but many believe official figures are inaccurate and the public are deliberately being kept in the dark.

"At the moment, the political preference is to not let the public understand what is happening," said Matteo Villa, head of the migration programme at the Institute for International Political Studies in Italy. "This way... the government doesn't run the risk of controversies over pushbacks or deaths at sea."

Until 2017, NGO rescue boats were co-ordinated by the Italian coastguard. Rescued migrants were taken to Italy because they wouldn't be safe if returned to Libya, where civil wars have raged since 2011.

But as arrivals in Italy hit record numbers, public opinion turned against refugees and political support for them fell away. In 2017, the EU supported Italy's then centre-left government to strike a deal with Libya, under which the EU provided funds, ships and training to the Libyan coastguard. In return, Libya intercepted fleeing migrants – between 15,000 and 30,000 – and took them back to its ports.

Critics, including Romaniuk, say the Libyans weren't answering distress calls, and there are reports that migrants and asylum seekers taken back to Libya have been tortured, raped or sold as slaves.

SOS Méditerranée, who operated the Aquarius with Médecins sans Frontières, told Euronews that if an NGO or a commercial boat rescued migrants in international waters and returned them to Libya, it would constitute a violation of international law.

In August that year, Italy asked all NGO

For governments who want us not to talk any more, the best way is for us not to be there

rescue boats working from its ports to sign a code of conduct. Regional prosecutors then launched investigations into them. Virtually all were unsuccessful, but when boats were kept-from the sea, some began to pull out.

SOS Méditerranée spokesperson Laura Garel for, said: "I guess, for governments who want us not to talk any more, the best way is for us not to be there."

In June 2018, Salvini announced on Twitter that Italy would close its ports to NGO rescue boats, and Gibraltar and Panama were pressured to revoke the registration of the Aquarius.

By the end of the year, no NGO rescue boats remained in the central Mediterranean. Only commercial operations, military vessels and the Italian and Libyan coastguard were left.

Most of their communications are confidential and observers can only discover basic information from the shore: how many leave Libya; how many arrive in Italy; how many are returned.

Villa says the figures on deaths at sea have become less reliable. After June 2018, deaths almost doubled, only to inexplicably nosedive soon after. The International Organisation of Migration says the drop is at least in part due to a dramatic fall in departures from Libya. Though some believe

smaller boats are still travelling without detection, meaning deaths also go unreported.

Sporadic reports offer a glimpse of what we may be missing. In September 2018, the deaths of more than 100 people were discovered, and in January 2019, after months in which few deaths were recorded, an Italian plane spotted a distressed boat carrying 120 people. When a helicopter arrived hours later, only three could be saved.

Another report revealed that a commercial boat under the Gibraltar flag returned 54 people to Libya in March.

Italy was persuaded to start search-and-rescue operations after a public outcry following hundreds of deaths in October 2013. Ultimately, not knowing what happens offshore reduces the chance of there being another.

"There is this idea of sweeping everything underneath the carpet without the public being aware," said Romaniuk. "But the problem is not going away." ⊗

Alessio Perrone is an Italian freelance journalist

ABOVE: Migrants hoping to cross over to Italy are spotted by the aid organisation SOS Méditerranée in January, 2018. Independent rescue boats are being forced out of sea by political deals

Standing up for freedom

After the murder of its mayor, **Adam Reichardt** says, Gdańsk is pushing back against government plans to rein in its spirit

48(01): 68/69 I DOI: 10.1177/0306422019841323

IN THE WAKE of mayor Paweł Adamowicz's assassination, the response in Gdańsk was one of solidarity.

His body lay in state for 24 hours at the European Solidarity Centre (ECS), before being transported to St Mary's Basilica, and an estimated 50,000 people queued for hours in the bitter cold to pay their respects.

It was no coincidence that Adamowicz's body was first laid out at ECS, one of his flagship projects. Officially launched in 2007, the centre opened in 2014 on the grounds of the former Lenin Shipyards – the birthplace of the Solidarity movement.

ECS is a museum, an archive, an open space for local citizens, and an office space for the former Polish president and leader of Solidarity, Lech Wałęsa. It is a symbol of the city's history of protest and openness.

It is not surprising either that the government wanted to cut large amounts of funding from the centre and then get the city to sack of some of its key staff.

After the killing Gdańsk, led by acting mayor Aleksandra Dulkiewicz, responded by launching a civic movement to raise the money through a crowdfunding campaign on Facebook and donations.

In 48 hours the campaign brought in the equivalent of $1.7 million – more than twice the amount of the missing funding. The city of Gdańsk had once again drawn on its protest spirit and became a centre of Polish defiance against the government.

Adamowicz's murder, on 14 January 2019, sent shockwaves which were felt across Poland and beyond. Such a brutal act, carried out during the finale of a charitable event and in front of crowds of hundreds of people, illustrates just how toxic the political environment is in Poland today.

On many occasions he embodied that spirit, standing in opposition to national trends and policies. Gdańsk agreed to accept refugees to the city despite the national government's refusal to participate in the EU's relocation programme. And the city later developed the first refugee integration programme of its kind, which became a model for other Polish cities willing to follow its bold lead.

Adamowicz was a frequent target of attacks in government-supported media, largely because he was a strong opponent of the populist policies of the ruling Law and Justice party. There is little doubt as to the political motivations of the murderer, an ex-convict who rushed the stage wielding a military-grade knife and who announced after the attack that Adamowicz was paying the price for his imprisonment, which had taken place under the previous Civic Platform government.

The mayor had cultivated the idea of Gdańsk being a "free city" – a reference back to the Free City of Danzig, as the city and surrounding area was known from 1920 to 1939.

Gdańsk is also particularly sensitive to meddling from the current government in its interpretation of history. A scandal erupted regarding the newly opened Museum of the Second World War. The original narrative of the museum had focused on the war from a

BELOW: Mourners pay respects to murdered mayor of Gdańsk Paweł Adamowicz, who was assassinated during a charity event in 2019

CREDIT: (left) Omar Marques/SOPA Images/LightRocket via Getty; (right) Chris Niedenthal/The LIFE Images Collection/Getty

global perspective, presenting it with the understanding that it broke out, at the peninsula in the city, Westerplatte, but had much wider consequences, affecting the lives of millions around the world.

The new government did not approve of this approach, arguing that it should be first and foremost focused on Polish victimhood. The government sacked the director and began to delicately reconfigure the museum's exhibition.

The ECS project also clashed with the official historical narrative of the Law and Justice party. The government interprets the roundtable talks of 1989 – negotiations between the Solidarity opposition movement and the communist government which led to the transition to democracy and the fall of the Berlin Wall – as a lost opportunity for Poland and one which it seeks to repair today.

It argues that many of the leading characters highlighted at the ECS main exhibition, such as Wałęsa, Tadeusz Mazowiecki, Bronisław Geremek and Andrzej Wajda, are the ones responsible for abandoning Poland's conservative national values and that the exhibit's narrative is blatantly one-sided.

Gdańsk is not a city to quietly obey diktats from Warsaw. Its heritage of protest and standing up to the authorities is in its DNA and spans generations. The famous shipyard strikes of the 1970s and 1980s, which led to the birth of the Solidarity movement, were the first

cracks which eventually led to the downfall of the communist system in Poland.

Even though the Solidarity movement was quashed with the imposition of martial law in 1981, Gdańsk remained a hotbed of pro-democracy opposition, publishing and distributing underground press to workers and intellectuals alike. As a result, communism finally collapsed in 1989. This year there will be celebrations to mark the 30th anniversary of those events.

This autumn will surely be a major test for Polish democracy when parliamentary elections will take place. From today's perspective, it seems that the ruling party faces an uphill battle. The opposition has shown signs that it is starting to gain some strength in the polls while the emergence of a new centre-left force called Wiosna (Spring) has raised the eyebrows of many Poles looking for something new.

The question remains whether the rest of the country will follow the example of Gdańsk and stand up against the government's populistic, interventionist tendencies. ⊗

ABOVE: In 1980 Polish Solidarity leader Lech Wałęsa addressed striking workers at Lenin shipyard in Gdańsk

In a matter of 48 hours, the campaign brought in the equivalent of $1.7million – more than twice the amount of the missing funding

Adam Reichardt *lives in Kraków, often works in Gdańsk, and is the editor-in-chief of the journal New Eastern Europe*

SPECIAL FEATURE

After the purge

In this special feature, we ask two writers to look back at what happened in Czechoslovakia in 1969 when it was under occupation by Soviet-led forces and to discuss what is happening to freedoms in Slovakia today. **Samuel Abrahám,** who fled Czechoslovakia as a teenager after the Soviets invaded, considers the challenges to media freedom and democracy and **Miriam Sherwood,** the granddaughter of satirist Ján Kalina, talks about her show and reflects on his work and her concerns about his homeland

SPECIAL FEATURE

Fifty years after 1969: what next?

Samuel Abrahám, who fled Czechoslovakia after the Soviet invasion, reflects that his country is now at a turning point

48(01): 70/73 I DOI: 10.1177/0306422019841324

ONE YEAR AFTER the murder of investigative journalist Ján Kuciak and his fiancée, Martina Kušnírová, the fight "for a decent Slovakia" is far from over.

The continual wave of protests following this heinous act unleashed energy and democratic fervour that surprised many who had been sceptical about Slovakia's willingness to stand up against the populist and corrupt political establishment.

Three weeks after the murder, Prime Minister Robert Fico was forced to resign as the protests gained intensity. There were repeated attempts to suppress the investigation but a trail leading to Fico's office made his position untenable.

His clumsy attempt to imitate Viktor Orbán's strategy in Hungary by portraying philanthropist George Soros as being behind the protests backfired, leaving him ridiculed. Moreover, during 2018, police and the courts finally exposed some of the politically connected corruption, and a few perpetrators have been tried and convicted. Previously, those accused of corruption had been exonerated by the system.

Thus Slovakia in 2019 seems somewhat more hopeful, in contrast with grim developments in neighbouring Hungary and Poland, yet the country is at a crossroads - and not

for the first time. It was in a similar quandary before. Half a century ago, it was not clear whether any reforms from 1968 would be preserved. In 1969, a purge by the new administration extinguished hopes of reforms, silenced the press and forced society to remain docile until the Velvet Revolution two decades later.

Could Slovakia learn a lesson from 1969? Could that failure indicate the direction this small and tested central European country might take in 2019?

In August 1968, Slovakia, then part of Czechoslovakia, was invaded by its Warsaw Pact "allies". It was a shock for all of us because we believed that "socialism with a human face", as the reforms of 1968 had been called, had been positive and progressive.

The reforms of the Prague Spring, led by Alexander Dubček, a Slovak, were quashed, and there was a Soviet-sponsored restoration of communist "normalcy", led by another Slovak, Gustav Husák, who supervised the purge. The political leadership and the population facing Leonid Brezhnev's Soviet Union had been much too naive: an empire cannot allow "socialism with a human face".

The protests following the invasion a Gandhi-type resistance, although initially →

The country is at a crossroads - and not for the first time. It was in a similar quandary before

→ marked by violence, gradually failed to sustain momentum. Odd as it might sound today, we believed that through protests we could force the occupiers out.

The most significant development was the gradual silence and censorship of the media, which had initially been quite free and outspoken against the invasion. Eventually, the censored media was transformed into the voice of the occupiers, and the population became lost and misinformed.

In fact, the main message of Jan Palach – who self-immolated in Wenceslas Square, Prague, in January 1969 – was to appeal to his fellow citizens to resist and sustain the togetherness against the occupiers. His funeral and our mourning was the second blow to Czechs and Slovaks. We felt betrayed and powerless. The feeling of mass humiliation invaded our national consciousness.

One could argue that the prolonged resistance and protests of 2018 were an echo of that failed historical resistance. Even though these protests were organised by the younger generation, all generations have been present in public squares, as if to say: "We do not want to be humiliated by ruthless politicians again."

At the time of his murder and that of his fiancée, Kuciak was investigating the corrupt activities of the Italian mafia in Slovakia, allegedly in collusion with criminals and Slovak politicians, and most notably in relation to the misuse of EU funds. The first reaction of senior politicians and the national police chief was to trivialise the murders, suggesting that it might have been the action of a drugs dealer they were doing business with.

With startling vulgarity, Fico, the then prime

minister, turned up at a press conference with €1 million in cash (the equivalent of $1.1 million), supposedly as a reward that would be paid for information leading to the arrest of the perpetrators. The public was shocked.

The next day, in an act of solidarity, all the main newspapers published Kuciak's unfinished article; the trail he had been following led, among other destinations, directly to the prime minister's office. Kuciak's article revealed how former topless model Maria Trošková was employed as an "adviser" in that office. She had no qualifications to be a political adviser to the prime minister and, in addition, Kuciak revealed that Trošková was a business partner and perhaps a mistress of an Italian mafia associate, Antonino Vadala.

It was Kuciak's article and Fico's bizarre press conference, with its mafia-style cash on the table, that led a handful of young students to organise protests calling for a proper investigation of the murders, and into suspicions of widespread corruption in Slovakia. Students Karolína Farská and Juraj Šeliga became the symbols of the protest movement *Za slušné Slovensko* (For a decent Slovakia) that organised protests by tens of thousands of people in every major Slovak city. The protests did not cease after Fico's resignation in 2019, continuing as the coalition government led by his party remained in office.

The movement used social media to organise the protests. But it was the free press that sustained the momentum during 2018 through a continual exposure of political corruption and the inaction of state institutions that were supposed to uphold the rule of law.

In addition, the investigation of the murders continued in earnest as the police were freed from the shackles of political interference. As a result, the murderers have been caught and businessman Marian Kočner, has been arrested and charged with ordering both murders.

Kočner had been exposed in numerous articles by Kuciak as a mafia-style criminal and embezzler, colluding with politicians, police and a former chief prosecutor. He was well connected with politicians in every administration and, before his arrest, had been protected from

Even though these protests were organised by the younger generation, all generations have been present in public squares

within the highest political circles. We can only hope that his trial will start the widespread exposure of political corruption.

The experience of 2018 and the memory of past struggles, defeats and victories provide some hope that Slovakia can continue to resist the forces of populism and nationalism. However, anti-immigrant sentiment appears to be shared by a large segment of the public and promoted by politicians.

Slovak society's first liberating and then tragic experience during 1968-69 provides a lesson for 2019. Civil society in Slovakia has steadily learned from its past defeats. And after the overthrow of its first post-communist strongman, Vladimír Mečiar, in 1998, there seems to be energy and momentum today to

end the era of Fico. The pressure from outside has always been taken seriously in Slovakia. Critical statements about the circumstances of Kuciak's murder by prominent Western media organisations are of utmost importance.

We can but hope that Slovakia, the bête noire of central Europe in the 1990s, could become a beacon of hope and an example for others now facing political crises on both sides of the former Iron Curtain. ⊗

Samuel Abrahám is based in Bratislava, Slovakia, and editor of Kritika & Kontext. He is rector of Bratislava International School of Liberal Arts

SPECIAL FEATURE

Banned laughter

Ján Kalina's book One Thousand and One Jokes was censored in Czechoslovakia in 1969. Granddaughter **Miriam Sherwood** explains why she is reviving his jokes and taking them home

48(01): 73/75 | DOI: 10.1177/0306422019841325

THE POLICE OFFICER asks the publisher: "Isn't it true that Ján Ladislav Kalina forced you to include politically subversive jokes in his book, One Thousand and One Jokes?" "Well, yes, he did," replies the publisher. "But they weren't as bad as the ones we didn't include."

This is part of the transcript from the trial interrogations of Ján Kalina, my granddad. He was a satirist and a prolific writer of cabarets

and radio programmes. His friends called him Laco. He was Jewish and survived the Holocaust thanks to the popularity of his work for Slovak. He thrived in the early years of communist post-war Czechoslovakia, opening the first permanent cabaret theatre in Bratislava and publishing his collection, One Thousand and One Jokes (Tisíc a jeden vtip).

Eventually, though, his way with words, combined with his Jewishness, got him into trouble. He was arrested by the secret police as the regime was clamping down on freedom of expression after the Prague Spring.

Now I have found myself following in my grandfather's footsteps, improving my Slovak in order to research and write a show about his life so that his story and his jokes can be heard again.

My mother, Julia, is at it too. She is working on a 50th anniversary edition of One Thousand and One Jokes, and what has struck us both is that the most insidious and damaging punishment for my grandfather was how successfully he was written out of Slovak history.

We believe that it is important to tell this story again at a time when my mum and →

Clearly, the communist regime subscribed to George Orwell's famous edict that "every joke is a tiny revolution" – even if it couldn't exactly pinpoint why this was the case

BELOW: Miriam Sherwood performing in her play Rendezvous in Bratislava

→ her friends observe a growing nostalgia for the communist regime in Slovakia, a rise in corruption and anti-semitism, and an increase in the susceptibility of young people to propaganda.

One Thousand and One Jokes was almost ready for publication in 1968 before the Russian tanks rolled into Czechoslovakia. At first, my granddad's response was to add a brand-new section of jokes about the Soviet invasion. But as censorship increased, he took them out and managed to get the book past the censors.

CREDIT: (below and right) Miriam Sherwood

It was published in June 1969 and sold out in less than two months, before the regime could ban it.

In 1972, he was arrested. He was in prison for nine months while they worked out what they could charge him with. In the end, he was found guilty of incitement: for having the intention to publish a book of political jokes abroad.

Clearly, the communist regime subscribed to George Orwell's famous edict that "every joke is a tiny revolution", even if it couldn't exactly pinpoint why this was the case. The secret police files from my granddad's case include a detailed "expert analysis" of One Thousand and One Jokes, which itself reads like satire.

Laco and his family were eventually given permission to emigrate in 1979. My grandma, Ági, went on to work for Radio Free Europe, while my mum finally fulfilled her plan to go to university. My mum eventually moved to London, where she began working for Amnesty International, an organisation that was instrumental in Laco's release from prison. She worked there for more than 20 years, campaigning for prisoners of conscience around the world and, after 1989, helping to set up Amnesty groups in eastern and central Europe and the former Soviet Union.

I never met Laco – he died eight years before I was born. But, luckily for me, he left behind a four-part autobiography (he

actually wrote a fifth, but it was confiscated by the secret police and never returned) and countless scripts, photo albums and scrapbooks.

As a theatre-maker, I couldn't help myself. I began to work on turning his life into a cabaret of its own. In the process, I've learnt to love the sound of his voice, his wit, his tenacity and, most of all, his conviction in the power and importance of laughter, theatre and entertainment, whatever the circumstances.

My "granddad cabaret" is called Rendezvous in Bratislava, after one of Laco's own shows, and last year was performed around England. I hope we'll be touring in Slovakia this autumn, where people are fighting once more for freedom of speech and respect for human rights. I'm sure my granddad would support this fight today. ✖

Miriam Sherwood *is a playwright and producer living in London*

ABOVE: (left) a poster for Miriam Sherwood's play Rendezvous in Bratislava; (right) a poster for Randezvous v Bratislave, the cabaret written by her grandfather, the satirist Ján Kalina

Fakebusters strike back

Raymond Joseph investigates deep fakes and gives advice on spotting this disturbing trend

48(01): 76/79 | DOI: 10.1177/0306422019841326

A BASIC INTERNET SEARCH for "deep fakes" plus the names of actresses Daisy Ridley, Emma Watson and Scarlett Johansson or singers Katy Perry and Taylor Swift is decidedly not safe for viewing at work.

It returns multiple hits from a wide variety of pornography websites of these famous women allegedly involved in a variety of kinky and shocking sex acts.

But not one of these videos is genuine. They are all fakes of varying degrees of sophistication, created with free – and freely-available – software used to substitute their faces on the bodies of actual porn actresses.

Welcome to the world of deep fakes – a portmanteau of "deep learning" and "fake" – which uses machine learning and artificial intelligence to create videos portraying people saying or doing things they never said or did.

It is not the first time that the multi-billion-dollar porn industry has taken the lead in creating or mainstreaming new tech, including e-commerce, webcams and streaming video. Deep-fake pornography first surfaced on the internet in 2017 when videos were posted on Reddit by a user under the pseudonym "Deepfakes".

The trickle of deep-fake hardcore porn videos soon turned into a deluge with the release of free software that made them relatively easy for anyone with a basic understanding of artificial intelligence to create. The problem became so serious that several platforms, including Reddit and Twitter, banned them. Late last year, Google also cracked down, adding "involuntary synthetic pornographic imagery" to its ban list and allowing anyone falsely depicted in them as "nude or in a sexually explicit situation" to request searches to the content be blocked.

So common has celebrity deep-fake porn become that actress Scarlett Johansson told the Washington Post: "Clearly this doesn't affect me as much because people assume it's not actually me in a porno, however demeaning it is. I think it's a useless pursuit legally, mostly because the internet is a vast wormhole of darkness that eats itself. The fact is that trying to protect yourself from the internet and its depravity is basically a lost cause, for the most part."

But dismissing online deep fakes as just something in the world of porn ignores the very real potential for them to be deployed on the mainstream web and in politics, taking online misinformation and disinformation to a new level.

You need only think of the damaging and divisive role played by social media in the US and other elections, and Brexit, to realise the potential damage well-crafted deep fakes could cause. In fragile democracies divided by strongman politics and cultural and tribal divides, the potential for using them to stir up hate and violence is a very real possibility.

Deep fakes are yet to be widely deployed "in the wild" beyond the world of porn, although there is a trend, which began as a meme on social media and went viral, of

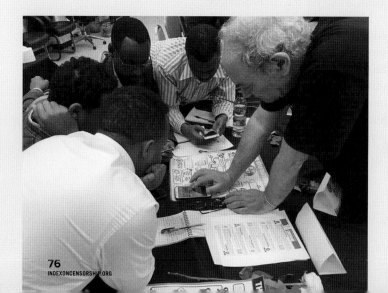

BELOW: Raymond Joseph teaches Ethiopian journalists how to spot fake photos

TIPS TO HELP YOU IDENTIFY DEEP-FAKE VIDEOS

||||||||||||||||||||||||||||||||||||||||||||||

Deep fakes have statistical patterns that make them algorithmically identifiable by machines. But the technology used to produce them is constantly improving and, over time, issues making them possible to identify will be smoothed over

THERE ARE WAYS, for now, to help you identify a deep fake.

1 Do a search to see if anyone else is reporting on the content of a video
2 Rely on trusted sources. Be wary of unknown people posting videos. They may be up to mischief, or just sharing them without checking
3 Take screen grabs from the video, then do a reverse image search to try to find the original video or photos
4 Apply common sense. Ask yourself would Barack Obama really make a video in which he calls Donald Trump a "dipshit"? And, if he did, would it go unreported by credible media?
5 Would movie stars at the height of their fame suddenly get involved in low-budget porn videos? In deep-fake pornos of famous actresses, you'll find multiple different kinds of body shapes for the same person in different videos

6 Do the journalism and vigorously fact-check to find supporting facts and corroborating sources
7 Does the location of any video make sense?
8 If a video of a speech is real, there's a good chance that credible media would have reported, and possibly videoed, it. Did they report it or post videos? Search for a transcript of the speech to compare against the video you are checking
9 Search some of the more outrageous statements to check if they were actually made by the person in the video

Here are some giveaway signs to look for in a manipulated deep-fake video (based on tips by artist and coder Kyle McDonald). Check out his blog at www.medium.com/@kcimc for example photos and additional tips and details

1 Straight hair, especially long hair, often looks like it's been painted
2 Check for background text: Generative Adversarial Networks, a form of AI used to create deep fakes, concentrate on faces and have difficulty in modelling writing
3 The background of a deep-fake video is messy
4 Eyes are often different sizes, cross-eyed and different colours. The same applies to ears and earrings, which are often different sizes and don't match
5 Teeth can be misaligned, with individual teeth stretched or shrunken in unusual ways
6 Hair in deep fakes is typically bunched in clumps, creates random wisps around the shoulders, and throws thick stray hairs onto foreheads

superimposing the face of the US actor Nicolas Cage onto the heads of other actors in popular movies. And another recent viral video created by actor-director Jordan Peele of former US President Barack Obama saying things he never said – such as that current President Donald Trump is a "dipshit" – highlighted the potential of deep fakes being used to spread disinformation … and worse.

But fakes don't need to be deep to be dangerous. Last year the White House shared a video after a confrontation between CNN's Jim Acosta and Trump that tried to alter what actually happened. The poorly doctored video attempted to make it appear that the veteran reporter had attacked an intern trying to wrest a microphone from him.

Concerned that deep fakes may be a threat to national security, several Congressmen have asked US intelligence authorities to investigate and report on their possible impact.

For journalists, let alone ordinary users, →

Dismissing online deep fakes as just something in the world of porn ignores the very real potential for them to be deployed on the mainstream web and in politics, taking online misinformation and disinformation to a new level

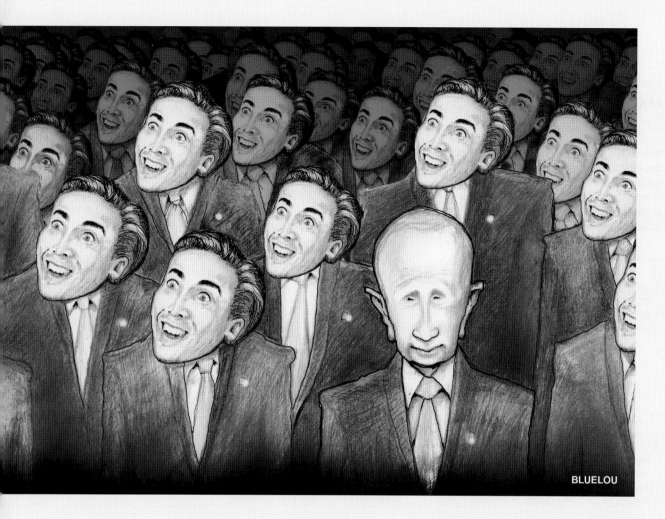

BLUELOU

→ already having to navigate the proliferation of misinformation, disinformation, hoaxes and assorted fakery swilling around online, debunking deep fakes raises the ante to a frightening new level. Leading experts say that although deep fakes are not yet a big problem, they could become one in the future.

And they agree that even though powerful tools will emerge to help identify deep fakes, the role of journalists doing traditional fact-checking and verification are key weapons in combating them.

Researchers and developers around the world are working furiously to build tools that will help to identify deep fakes.

The US military has already developed a tool to identify them, although it is not commercially available. And Carnegie Mellon University researcher Satya Venneti has had some success with a tool that analyses the pulses and blood flows of people in videos to help identify fakes.

Claire Wardle, the head of research at First Draft News and a leading expert on verification, says that while deep fakes need to be watched, she is not disproportionately worried by them.

"I'm more worried about all the news coverage of it, much of which is fearmongering. It's potentially going to lead to people not trusting anything they see," she said.

"We do have pretty sophisticated tools to verify images and videos that have been honed over the last decade of doing things like verifying YouTube videos of chemical weapons attacks in Syria. That is also really hard. There are also many very smart academics working on tools to detect deep fakes so by the time they are a real problem I feel confident we will have tools to fight back."

Journalists will have to use all the same skills they've always used, she says.

"Is there supporting evidence to suggest this event took place? Does the location make sense? What does the transcript of the speech say? What did witnesses say?"

Ben Nimmo, a senior fellow for information defence at the Atlantic Council's Digital Forensic Research Lab, was at the forefront of unmasking Russian bots that interfered in the US 2016 elections.

"At the moment, we haven't seen [deep fakes] used," he said. "The Russian government has run plenty of shallow fakes (such as manipulated images) which have been caught out. Deep fakes would be yet another escalation in the information warfare. It's probably only a matter of time."

Deep fakes, he says, are a risk because they could lead to journalists making mistakes. They must be aware of the problem and always look for corroborating sources.

"Ultimately, though, they'll need to develop a stronger relationship with the tech platforms, who have the best technical expertise and who have a big stake in not letting their platforms be taken over by fakes."

He also has a stark warning: "If you wait for the lies to come, you'll be too late. The media need to educate themselves, and the public, in how to predict all sorts of fakes and disinformation. For example, the Russian government always uses the same four techniques: dismiss, distort, distract and dismay. Teaching people to spot those are the best way of helping them to protect themselves."

Peter Cunliffe-Jones, executive director of fact-checking organisation Africa Check, believes that deep fakes present a serious challenge to journalists.

"They need – first of all – to be aware of the problem," he said. "[In] the run-up to the elections in Nigeria and Senegal, Africa Check saw many media simply relaying content that was false or faked. The first thing for any editor to do with shocking or surprising content is to ask a series of questions about its source and origin – and that goes for video, too.

"Fortunately, deep fakes appear still to be quite rare at present. But that does not mean that they can be discounted. And in fragile societies, deep-fake videos hitting a nerve on sensitive topics have the potential to sow real

There is a trend, which began as a meme on social media and went viral, of superimposing the face of the US actor Nicolas Cage onto the heads of other actors in popular movies

violence or undermine due process."

Analyst Kyle Findlay played a key role in identifying the so-called Guptabots deployed as part of a campaign by British PR agency Bell Pottinger. The Guptabots were social media accounts run to discredit critics of the then South African president Jacob Zuma and his friends. They were named after the Gupta brothers who were accused of having a corrupt relationship with Zuma. The bots helped sow racial tensions in the country by accusing critical journalists of spreading a "white monopoly capital" narrative.

"For now, deep fakes have statistical patterns present in them that make them identifiable by machines," said Findlay. "Over time, these might be smoothed over by the makers. For now, though, in some cases there are ways of identifying them algorithmically."

He says the war against deep fakes "will turn into an evolutionary arms race. Tools for detection will arise and be circumvented".

He added: "We might need to supply journalists with automated 'image provenance' tools, like the plug-ins that you use for reverse image search to automatically trace back the 'share' trail of all media to their sources."

But his advice is ultimately non-technical and encourages the use of good old-fashioned journalism.

"Treat everything with suspicion. Focus on names you trust and insist on visible trails linking the media that you are viewing back to those trusted sources." ⊗

Raymond Joseph *is a South African journalist, based in Cape Town*

Cover up

Charlotte Bailey talks to Kuwaiti writer **Layla AlAmmar** about the 4,000 books banned in her country, many like hers about women

48(01): 80/82 I DOI: 10.1177/0306422019841327

KUWAIT'S FIRST #METOO novel is set to be banned in its own country. As Index went to press, it was still unclear if Layla AlAmmar's debut novel, The Pact That We Made, a story of a woman who has been sexually assaulted and attempts by her parents to cover it up, would be allowed in bookshops.

In Kuwait books are reviewed by a committee working for the ministry of information, which prepares one-page reports flagging content considered offensive. Last autumn, in response to a request from a member of parliament, the government published a list of all the books that had been forbidden since 2014. There were more than 4,000. The list included the book of the Disney version of The Little Mermaid, because the mermaid – who wears a bikini top – was deemed too scantily clad.

It is, therefore, not surprising that a young female writer discussing taboo topics might be concerned that her book would never be sold in her home country. Even before she wrote the novel, AlAmmar was a campaigner against the bans, writing passionate blogs and articles. But her own work and ambition were never at the top of her list of concerns.

"I was not thinking about my own book. The first thing that came to my mind was 'this is insane, and we, as a freethinking society, cannot tolerate it'," she said.

The sexual assault AlAmmar describes in her

novel happens long before the story starts, but it is clear the trauma, exacerbated by the way it is dealt with by her parents, is having a debilitating effect on the central character's everyday life.

During a conversation with one of her closest friends, the protagonist Dahlia, asks herself: "How could I explain to her that nothing in my life felt real? That in a country like Kuwait, where everyone knew everything about each other, the most monumental thing to ever happen to me was buried and covered over?"

This story follows Dahlia, who is on the brink of turning 30 in a very traditional society and struggling under immense pressure to marry. As the novel progresses, it becomes clear that her sense of self is being eroded until, ultimately, she has to decide if she has it in her to make her own choices – and if her voice matters.

The book bans, which have affected much literature about women and their experiences, came as a shock particularly to Kuwait's intellectuals and writers who were proud of its reputation as a cultural oasis during the 1970s and 1980s, when it was relatively free compared with the rest of the Gulf and some parts of the wider Middle East.

"Kuwait was seen as an intellectual haven for people to express themselves," said Ebtehal Alkhateeb, assistant professor of literature at the University of Kuwait. #Banned_In_Kuwait and #Dont_Decide_For_Me have trended on Twitter, while activists have protested on the streets and expressed their anger online.

Writers who have had their work banned

I try to maintain the idea that liberalism is not a Western idea but a human idea

ABOVE: A family attend the 43rd international book fair in Kuwait City, November 2018

have felt it personally. Mai Al-Nakib, associate professor of literature at Kuwait University, saw her book, The Hidden Light of Objects, banned four years after its publication. She said: "I felt sad. In many ways, my book is a kind of lopsided love letter to Kuwait. That it would be banned here does break my heart a little."

Paradoxically, analysts say that the ban is a consequence of a democratic process rather than autocracy. Kuwait is what analysts call "a partial democracy". A constitutional emirate, the country's executive power is held by a hereditary emir – currently Sabah al-Ahmad al-Jaber al-Sabah. This leader dominates the judiciary and appoints the prime minister, but the elected parliament has influence and often challenges the government. The pressure for the ban comes from the largely conservative elected parliament.

One analyst based in the region explains that in recent years there have been two simultaneous trends, saying: "More and more young people [are] testing and pushing red →

ABOVE: Kuwaiti novelist Layla AlAmmar

I felt sad. In many ways, my book is a kind of lopsided love letter to Kuwait. That it would be banned here does break my heart a little

→ lines – often crossing them – [and] the government has become both more willing to enforce the rules and better at doing so.”

This puts a chill on political debate and contributes to a feeling that there is less space for freedom of expression in Kuwait. Several media outlets have been punished for their coverage of the regime and the newspaper Al-Watan, which was often critical of the government, is still closed following its suspension in 2015.

Even if AlAmmar’s book is banned, it will still be easily accessed on e-readers, along with most of the other forbidden books. “It’s not about getting the books,” Alkhateeb said. “The government is making a political statement through banning these books.”

Because the books can still be accessed and read, AlAmmar says she did not see the level of outrage that she expected. “A lot of people weren’t even aware of it. Or they said ‘oh well, who cares if they ban 4,000 books, nobody buys their books from here anyway’,” she said.

Similarly, Alkhateeb reports that many of the

students she teaches are not particularly upset by the ban. “They say they are against the ban but... I say as soon as you introduce the word ‘but’ you have lost the battle. The principle of freedom of expression cannot be given up,” she said. “To me, censorship is a life or death kind of situation. Once you accept the principle itself you are taking everything that comes with it.”

One reason that people give for having some sympathy for the ban is that freedom of expression is seen as a Western concept.

“If you’re criticising anything, or you’re asking for freedom of expression or for no censorship, then you are copying the West or you are taking on Western ideas which have a conflict with our traditional ideas,” said AlAmmar.

And Alkhateeb agrees, saying: “They associate it with a society they see as too open, too free. I try to maintain the idea that liberalism is not a Western idea but a human idea.”

AlAmmar fiercely defends the principle of freedom of expression as a crucial and universal concept.

“Kuwait prides itself on being a democracy, but it should be remembered that democracy doesn’t begin and end with the ballot box. It extends as a mode of thought and a way of life that prizes plurality and tolerance,” she wrote in an opinion piece.

“The ability to read, and read critically, is a kind of magic.” ⊗

Charlotte Bailey is a journalist covering human rights and international development issues including for The Guardian, Time and BBC Radio 4

Silence speaks volumes

Tanzanian artists and musicians are the latest to be hit by bans and, as **Neema Komba** reports, new laws make it hard for anyone to speak out

48(01): 83/85 I DOI: 10.1177/0306422019841328

IN BAGAMOYO, A town not far from Dar es Salaam, artist Amani Abeid hangs his latest work, The Protected, ready for an exhibition. In his painting, a brilliant red umbrella adorned with yellow patterns hangs over a brown flower pot. The plants under the umbrella are brown, dying from the protection of the umbrella, while the plants outside it are thriving.

Amani's painting makes me think of the things that die because of good intentions.

This work is Amani's way of speaking out against the stifling of democracy and free speech that is happening in Tanzania. The country, which is gearing up for a general election in 2020, has been passing new regulations and amending laws to make it more difficult for opposing views to be expressed without legal repercussions. The Media Services Act, the online content regulations, the amendments to the Statistics Act, and the Political Parties Act all have elements that threaten freedom of speech, press freedom and democracy.

For artists such as Amani, the impact their work can have is at the mercy of the national arts council Baraza la Sanaa la Taifa (Basata). In 2018 the council passed 64 regulations making it difficult to create works of art. According to these regulations, all artists must register

themselves with Basata. This requires an artist to pay an initial registration fee and a yearly fee. Basata also censors artworks, music, film, theatre, and visual arts and crafts, before they can be consumed.

The censorship element has affected the music industry. Lyrics must be submitted and analysed before they can be played to the public. Artists, like hiphop star Diamond Platnumz, have had their songs banned for not submitting them, as well as for their content.

Basata may ban any artwork within its mandate that it deems offensive, it thinks may cause public discord or it judges to be contrary to Tanzanian morals under the guise of formalising the arts industry, promoting authentic Tanzanian traditions and protecting peace. "The current regime wants to be feared," Richard Mbunda, a political science lecturer at the University of Dar es Salaam, told Index.

However, a government, no matter how repressive, cannot silence all its citizens. Someone, somewhere, will speak out about something that matters to them, no matter the consequences. There will be brave Tanzanians out there – those who will go to war with their own fear and speak their truth.

Mbunda had to conquer his fear to write an open letter to President John Magufuli, as part of the co-ordinated effort to lobby against the introduction of genetically modified organisms in Tanzania.

"I took it as my responsibility to stand for the truth, as a researcher and as a son of smallholder farmers," he said. While that letter was his first, he wasn't afraid to sign his name at the end.

While some GMO proponents had labelled Mbunda as being anti-science, the Tanzanian community rallied behind him. His letter, which was published on the Tanzanian blog site Udadisi, went viral. The Tanzanian →

There will be brave Tanzanians out there – those who will go to war with their own fear and speak their truth

ABOVE: Top African popstar Diamond Platnumz performs in Kenya. He has been barred from performing in Tanzania after playing a song banned by the authorities

CREDIT: Daniel Irungu/REX/Shutterstock

smallholder farmers' network also issued a statement against the GMO trials. According to Mbunda, the trials weren't some cutting-edge science geared to help the Tanzanian farmer but business efforts of a multi-national company that would kill Tanzania's food sovereignty. The government, in response to the open letter, banned GMO trials in Tanzania. It was a great demonstration of how speaking out can pay off.

Yet despite his great win, Mbunda is not very optimistic about the state of free speech in Tanzania. As a researcher, he is deeply concerned by the Statistics Act, which outlaws any criticism of government-issued statistics. The law also gives the National Bureau of Statistics the power to censor independent and institutional researchers, greatly impairing their freedom. With laws such as this, how can Tanzania demand accountability from its elected government?

To speak out in a country that reveres silence, you must be ready to lose everything. Maxence Melo, founder of the Tanzanian networking site JamiiForums, has been facing intimidation at the hands of law enforcement, often getting arrested and questioned. The existence of the forum, which amplifies the voice of Tanzanians, seems to pose a threat to a government that prefers the silence of its citizens. Melo has been in a prolonged legal

battle since 2016 because he refuses to give up the identities of the whistleblowers. He is unable to leave the confines of Dar es Salaam without permission from a court. His passport has been confiscated. His financial status is in near ruin because advertisers are afraid of associating themselves with JamiiForums. Yet he presses on because the alternative is far too daunting. His friends are afraid to be seen with him. He presses on because the alternative is far too daunting.

The consequences of speaking out against those in power in Tanzania can be dangerous. In 2017, Tindu Lissu, an outspoken opposition leader from the centre-right party Chadema, was gunned down and left severely wounded. Lissu, who is still undergoing treatment in Belgium, maintains that the government is to blame for this assassination attempt.

I am wary to fully blame the silence of Tanzanians on the restrictive laws passed by the current administration. The culture of silence is deeply rooted in the Tanzanian community – in our families and our institutions. Vicensia Shule, a senior lecturer at the University of Dar es Salaam, recently found out how much silence was preferred in her institution when she spoke out publicly. She wrote a tweet to Magufuli, who was visiting the university to open a new library, calling out "corruption in the form of sexual favours" and saying it was rampant at the institution.

Shule had already been labelled a troublemaker for calling out injustices and fighting the gender pay gap in her department, and she was called to the ethics committee to answer for her statement. Her pending promotion from senior

In 2018 the council passed 64 regulations making it difficult to create works of art

lecturer to associate professor was put on hold, and friends and colleagues avoided her so that they would not be tainted. The institution has decided to silence her in order to make an example out of her and intimidate others like her from speaking out. But Shule refuses to be silenced or to normalise silence.

"We aren't supposed to criticise the institution. We are supposed to protect it by our silence. But to progress, we have to break the silence," she told Index, as I sat with her outside the University of Dar es Salaam *mama lishe* food stall. She didn't seem afraid, but she admitted she had to conquer her fear of death.

"Speaking out is a process," she said. "You don't just get a sudden courage to speak out against big things. We have to start speaking out against small stuff in a constructive manner."

We must acknowledge the difficulty of expressing oneself while constantly facing censorship at every corner. Many of those responsible for censorship might have good intentions – to save the face of our beloved Tanzania, to protect our precious peace, or to uphold traditions.

But, as we approach elections, I can't help but wonder how this censorship will be used against Tanzanian citizens. What will happen to those who publish polls about candidates and political parties? What statistics will the citizens be fed, and what will happen to those who question them? How many songs will be silenced before they hit the airwaves, and how many will be banned soon after?

And whatever it is we are protecting, does it survive under our umbrella of silence, or does it die? ⊗

Neema Komba *is an award-winning poet and writer from Tanzania*

RIGHT: A protest ended in a massacre when the Chinese army opened fire on students in Tianan-men Square, 1989

CULTURE

2019: the year of the troll?

Sally Gimson talks to Slovak novelist **Michal Hvorecký** about his battle for the truth

48(01): 88/93 I DOI: 10.1177/0306422019840153

LEFT: Award-winning novelist Michal Hvorecký

" **WHAT WE ARE** facing now in eastern Europe with trolling is the destruction of the belief in the free press. And we are not able to deal with 'fake news' becoming mainstream news." This is the gloomy conclusion of award-winning Slovak novelist and activist Michal Hvorecký.

His novel Troll, the opening of which we publish below, portrays a dystopian world where the country he describes, a thinly disguised Slovakia, is run by a dictatorship which retains control by employing internet trolls to pump out propaganda and conspiracy theories.

His two heroes decide to become trolls themselves to beat the system, with devastating consequences.

Hvorecký, 42, lives and works in Bratislava. He wrote the novel, which has not yet been translated into English, as a way of trying to understand the world he is living in today.

Since he wrote it, the Slovak journalist Ján Kuciak has been killed, more and more websites are pumping out misinformation and polls in Slovakia show anti-semitism is on the rise. He is frequently asked what the solution is to the increase in "fake news", but he does not know.

What he does know is that 2019 will be a crunch year for Slovakia, and presidential and European elections will show if the country has finally decided to back authoritarianism or if the people who believe in what he calls "Western values, the free world and democracy" will win the day.

"It is really falling dramatically, the support for a democratic Slovakia. We have now a rise of politicians who are clearly saying 'we are anti-system' – that's what makes them popular," he told Index. "I think 2019, where we have a lot of elections in Slovakia, and Europe as well, is going to be one of the decisive years for the near future."

Hvorecký blames Russian interference for the strength of anti-democratic movements in the country. He says Russian embassies in Prague and Bratislava are supporting anti-Nato, anti-EU billboard campaigns and news websites. It is young people who are susceptible and, he says, more supportive of populist parties than any other age group in the country. He mentions the international TV network RT as well as "alternative" news agency Sputnik, which are both Russian government-funded. He adds that the news site Hlavné Správy also pumps out pro-Russian propaganda.

"It's called Main News, which is a very clever title. They pretend to be a news portal like [the] BBC or CNN but they are actually only spreading propaganda and hate 24/7," he said. "It's a horrible page but it is the most popular 'fake news' site in Slovakia...they are clearly supporting a presidential candidate [Štefan Harabin] who is anti-democratic and anti-European, anti-Nato, pro-Russian, pro-Putin... They are of course anti-migrant, very pro-Orbán, pro-Hungarian prime minister. They have a very clear agenda and they are personally connected with Russian propaganda networks. They are not even hiding it anymore."

Hvorecký, who is a public figure in Slovakia, is inevitably the subject of much "fake news" himself. In December last year, he decided to challenge his trolls and wrote an email to each of the 70 people who had shared on social media a fabricated quote by him which suggested he wanted Isis to come to Slovakia. Ten people responded and three apologised, but Hvorecký said having a conversation

We have now a rise of politicians who are clearly saying 'we are anti-system' – that's what makes them popular

with them was impossible.

"You can't talk to these people. I tried to start some sort of dialogue and explain to them. They tried to say I was hired by [George] Soros to spread lies…. After five emails I gave up. You can't persuade them about anything. These people have faith, they are emotional about this. It's not rational. They don't want to hear you arguing with them…how can you start a dialogue when there is one side not listening?"

And his next book? It's a comic utopian novel, he says, called Tahiti

It is really falling dramatically, the support for a democratic Slovakia

about a 2018 world where Slovakia does not exist. The allies after World War I have allowed the formation of greater Hungary, and the Slovak population has emigrated to the Polynesian island of Tahiti.

Hvorecký said: "In my book, only the Czech Republic has existed for 100 years and there was never any

Slovakia. So when this is published, I think I will probably have to leave for exile because Slovaks will not be happy to read it." ⊗

Sally Gimson is the deputy editor at Index on Censorship

Troll

I am the most hated person on our local internet. Most people must have seen my mug by now. Crossed out or smeared with blood, my face is spreading on social media at a pace of ten thousand hates an hour. Not even the most hopeless football game or bruising defeat at hockey can stir up so much hatred. Not even our president and the prime minister. The winner of the Eurovision song contest who sang about some sad elephant in a jolly zoo is Miss Popularity compared to me. Opposition politicians and cabinet members are secretly grateful to me – at last people have channelled their hatred elsewhere.

Photos circulate on the net, attributing statements to me I've never made. But who would bother to check? Checking is something that used to be done at one time, a long, long time ago… In another galaxy. Checking is out. Retro, at best.

I'm a walking demotivational quote.

A meme.

An animated gif.

An informational facsimile.

The dreadful photos are spreading like digital wildfire. Among those who will spot the awful shots on the net will be Sarah Lutz. I was the one who'd dug them out after she appealed for solidarity with refugees. Even a cult figure like Sarah has never faced so many adversaries at once.

Now I have an inkling of what she must have felt.

Teeth bared, I scream for millions more refugees. With a half-witted grin, I call for Islamic State to attack Vienna and Warsaw. Eyes wide with excitement, I demand that all citizens turn gay and lesbian and end up looking like Conchita Wurst.

→ Although I've spent most of my life on the internet, I've never seen so many emoticons. I tried to respond on message boards. I posted comments. I fired off emails. I publicly pledged to send their creators snapshots that would be even more horrible. But their understanding of humour was about the same as mine of their actions.

I checked out the profiles of the people attacking me. In addition to a passion for shaven heads, the politics of the Reich, US motorcycles and Chinese vests, they have all graduated from the university of life.

They called me the most florid names: a Khazar Zionist, Soros's carbuncle, a Nazi Jew (sic!), a traitor to my homeland, a fascist, a disgrace to the nation, a disgrace to the world, a Russophile, an Americophile, a love-and-truth-freak, an Israeli, a Palestinian, a snowflake, butterball, an xxx (word automatically erased by software), a prize xxx (I get the drift), a circumcised xxx, a virgin (how did they know?), an agent of the West, an agent of the East, a gay cunt, a pseudo-intellectual, a pseudo-human being, NGO-scum, Havel (an insult?), a disgusting fatso.

It was almost as if I'd told them what to write.

I put on a black balaclava and infiltrated the crowd that chanted my name, demanding a public execution. This wasn't happening a hundred or five hundred years ago in some medieval market-place or prison camp but in the main square of the metropolis where I was born and have lived all my life.

I wasn't hallucinating. I was taking it all in with my senses sharpened. In the world around me facts didn't matter. Genuine anarchy in the UK. In Europe. In the US.

I walked the streets casting furtive looks around. The city felt ghost-like. The streets were teeming with people.

I was desperately looking for her in the crowd. I hoped we could meet again. Everything would be explained.

My heart was pounding. I was paralysed by fear. Outraged voices screamed my name so loud that my ears got blocked. They loathed me the way the Crusaders loathed blasphemers.

I could only edge ahead a few dozen metres at a time. Even this slow pace required a huge amount of energy. I was scared of being trampled to the ground.

The crowd geared up to lynch some other fatso in a balaclava. They thought they'd got me. At the last minute, he managed to reveal his face and save his life. It was a close shave.

Protesters were arriving from the farthest ends of the city. They crept out of their dark dens, dingy flats, cellars, bedsits and hovels. They got up from their computers, put down their tablets. They were hurtling along the streets like a swollen river.

Tens of thousands of Anonymous masks and balaclavas out in the open. Summoned by Google and Facebook, by algorithms based on previous searches and clicks.

The information war roused them from their computer solitude. It wasn't the truth they were looking for on the web but a shared worldview. Every new "like" increased their bias against me, corralling masses of them into like-minded groups and supplying them with the kind of gibberish they yearned for. They longed for confirmation that I was a tranny and a Jew. Though it wasn't true, it could easily have been.

Around the corner a shop window was on fire. The air quivered. Smoke billowed above the barricades. Some protesters wore ski goggles, others sported builders' hard hats and gas masks with skulls on them. I heard rhythmic banging on metal and drums.

The clothes on my back and shoulders were damp. Protesters dragged up a mannequin with my face and hung it from the gallows. A procession organised by the Institute of Unborn Children arrived. Pilgrims wearing cowls dragged floats plastered with billboards boasting blown-up

→

→ photos of abortions. They carried poles with dummy foetuses mounted on them, drenched in fake blood. They held up banners with slogans in Cyrillic script, grotesquely misspelt.

The Reich's Devils biker gang roared. It was followed by neo-Nazis marching in formation, and members of the radical left carrying banners with hammers and sickles, and portraits of the Leader-Father and the Leader-Son. Priests in vestments sang, their eyes raised heavenwards. Young men bearing sacrificial gifts and murmuring prayers hoisted church flags and enormous black crosses. The veiled monk Yevgeny Semionov was also there to greet the crowd. Next came a column of supporters of alternative and conspiracy media. A delegation of healers and naturopaths brought pendulums, spheres and a zapper. Veterans of the hybrid war threatened ferocious revenge.

At last, they all joined forces. They were united by their need to hate something that was alive, warm, close, ours, something tangible.

On the rostrum stood two men who read out an address by a fake Keanu Reeves. That is, by me.

I refuse to be a part of a world where men force women to wear clothes that make them look like prostitutes. Where there is no respect and the human word can't be trusted unless it also involves a promise. Where women don't want to bear children and men don't want to have families. Where young people think they've achieved something just because they drive their parents' cars, and those in power openly show that they don't give a damn about anyone else. Where hypocritical people profess their faith in God with a bottle of drink in their hand and without any clue about religion. Where everything is just blah-blah-blah because of blah-blah-blah in order to blah-blah-blah.

They hated me using my own words! A textbook example! At the end of the speech, the loudspeakers roared:

Wanna help the Reich? Don't be wanker trash!

Fight for what is ours: Tatras, Moscow, Urals!

Don't feed the troll, kick him out, score a goal!

Don't count on Sion or Soros, you bloody homos,

You tranny, you virgin, we'll send you lurchin',

You stoner, you snowflake, go to hell for your own sake,

We'll kick your ass, the bell will toll, is that what you want, you troll?

We'll string you up, hang you out to dry! Be up front, roll a joint,

Don't feed him nuthin', he ruins everythin',

He'd kill his own dad for a petrodollar,

Don't like, only diss, block, report and dismiss, screech at the bitch,

The Reich patrol will hunt down the troll,

Don't buy it, switch to Reddit,

Save your like for my mike, negate the Troll, lol, lol, lol!

Fatherland Crew are taking part in a rally against me? Anything is possible now.

All sorts of rude jokes about me went viral. I was the only one not sharing them.

I spotted a tabloid with my photo at a newsstand. I've taken the front page over from a famous MC who came out as gay even though he's married with three children. Online computer gamers could slap me in the face for free, kick me in the gut and, on reaching the final level, saw my head off.

Blood tickled my nostrils, I felt the hot liquid trickling down my throat. I spat and wiped my mouth with the back of my hand.

The protesters sprayed my best-known nicknames on the walls: Peter. Martin. Jakub. Damian. Ester. Nina. Martina. Eva. Jozef. Keanu. Sarah. Eighty names and counting. The real one is… I forget… I don't know… My name is… My name was… I was no longer sure what my name was. They have taken everything from me. I am a troll.

Yet all I wanted was to achieve my purpose. My plan. Our plan.

I tried to elbow my way out of the crush and retreat into safety. Mustn't attract attention.

Too late. I was surrounded. I looked for a gap to slip into but… I couldn't see an escape route, I had run out of energy and time. Think. What are your options? Get the hell out of here. Concentrate, breathe, you're not tired, you can make it. Where to? Anywhere.

They were marching towards me, in close array, like an army conquering a fortified castle. Without a word, in the kind of silence that often falls before an explosion. Their eyes blazed eerily.

I was scarpering off as fast as I could. Someone grabbed me by the shirt from behind.

"Take your mask off!"

Fair enough. It was to be expected. No escape.

My brother, Johana, my mother, the discussion boards, it all flashed through my mind. I wished I could stay offline and never be connected again. No more discussing, commenting, trolling.

Eyes filled with hostility were fixed on me. I looked around in panic. I hoped to see someone who might offer me shelter, put in a good word for me. Nothing. I had no real friends, only virtual ones generated by myself or other trolls. My mates = computer bots. They mimic real profiles and disseminate whatever I tell them to.

"Take his balaclava off, right now!" a male voice yelled.

Someone ripped off a piece of material.

The mute white mask they saw underneath shocked them. A smooth face, a shaved head. Featureless and expressionless, shapeless, a spitting image of the eggheads in Chirico's paintings.

"I have to speak to Johana, I have a vitally important message for her," I said. I sounded like the old Daft Punk on vocoder, rasping like a mortally wounded Darth Vader.

I no longer had a name, or voice, or face.

....

*Translated by **Julia Sherwood***

***Michal Hvorecký** is a Slovakian novelist and short story writer. His latest novel Troll was published in 2017 in Slovakian. His books have been translated into 11 languages. He is based in Bratislava, Slovakia*

Ghost writers

Index editor **Rachael Jolley** discusses Chinese state control with historian **Jeffrey Wasserstrom** 30 years after the Tiananmen Square massacre

48(01): 94/98 I DOI: 10.1177/0306422019840158

LEFT: Jeffrey Wasserstrom is a US author specialising in modern China

HISTORY IS SOMETHING that academic Jeffrey Wasserstrom regularly reviews, the future less so.

However, for his new short story for this magazine, California-based Wasserstrom takes an academic lecture of the future as his inspiration.

This lecture, delayed by superstorms hitting the world, takes place in 2049 and includes references to two of his favourite authors – Aldous Huxley and George Orwell.

Wasserstrom, who is a professor of history at the University of California, Irvine, has been a fan of Orwell – as well as other European writers and characters including George Bernard Shaw and Sherlock Holmes – since, as a teenager, he wrote a play featuring many of them as characters.

His interest in Orwell developed as his academic research on China gathered pace. His fascination with Huxley's Brave New World came later, when giving a guest lecture at a US college in 2003. He added: "Once I went into Chinese studies I was really interested that [Orwell]

had spent time in Burma, helping to shape his view that the dangers of an all-powerful state came partly from colonialism – it wasn't just about Stalin."

But by the mid-1990s and early 2000s, he says, China was in more of a Huxley phase with mega-malls and masses of entertainment.

"In the mid-80s it was a very boring place. By the 1990s you were just spoiled for choice... maybe Huxley is as valuable as Orwell, so I kept coming back to the two views of the future and how they fit with China."

Wasserstrom is also fascinated by how both Nineteen Eighty-Four and Brave New World are on sale in China without too much fuss.

"You can buy Nineteen Eighty-Four in bookshops in China, which my friends who study the Soviet Union think is kind of crazy. You couldn't buy it in Russia until right before communism was over.

"Orwell would think that was strange that his book was seen as so subversive...Huxley would say: 'Ha, it is a consumer good that

intellectuals like, so give intellectuals what they like – and as long as they stay off the street, what's the problem? Keep them reading'...

"And you can buy Brave New World Revisited as well: it just has the parts about China [marked] out. If it is not about China, anything goes to a certain extent."

Wasserstrom's fictional lecture takes place 100 years after an important historic document, a letter written in 1949 from Huxley to his former pupil, Orwell, after reading Nineteen Eighty-Four.

But that's not the only anniversary worth thinking about as we read Wasserstrom's fiction. The other is the 4 June commemoration of the killings at Tiananmen Square 30 years ago.

Does he think that there will be any protests this year, and will the Chinese government respond?

"I think there will be more watchfulness," he said, adding: "I think the fact that the world didn't pay all that much attention to Umbrella [a series of protests held in Hong Kong in 2014] helped embolden the government. Beijing always wanted to put more controls on Hong Kong but felt that they didn't want to pay the price for that earlier.

"But in the last few years they have felt with each step they have made that there hasn't been enough international outrage to stop them doing it more."

In other words, the Chinese government is getting less worried about international condemnation, and increasingly sees itself as free to crack down on protest or public expression of different kinds.

You can buy Nineteen Eighty-Four in bookshops in China, which my friends who study the Soviet Union think is kind of crazy

The Chinese government ... increasingly sees itself as free to crack down on protest or public expression of different kinds

"It is less vulnerable to international censure," he said, adding that he was struck by how much more China was concerned about its international reputation in 2008 when it was hosting its first Olympics. He added: "There are lots of ironies at the current moment. One irony is how

China and Russia both have strongman autocratic traditionalist leaders ... and here we have Russia post-communist, and China still communist, and yet [the] leaders of the two countries are chummier than the leaders of the two countries have been since the 1950s. In many ways their strategies

are parallel." The fact that the world is distracted right now, particularly the USA and the UK, means that there is even more space for the Chinese government to take tough measures, like their use of technology to impose a social credit system that monitors and ranks their citizens. They are able to take these measures almost without being noticed, and without consequences. ⊗

Rachael Jolley is editor of *Index on Censorship*

The Huxley Papers

Thoughts on the centenary of Nineteen Eighty-Four delivered by **Jeffrey Wasserstrom** at the Orwell Archive, UCL, London, UK, on 1 October, 2049

COLLEAGUES, IT'S AN honour to speak on the final evening of this conference commemorating the hundredth birthday of the book that introduced the terms "newspeak", "Big Brother", and "memory hole". The organisers have apologised for having to delay the symposium due to the terrible super-storms earlier this year that grounded all planes for weeks. (You'd think that by now, we would all be used to such things due to how common they became in the 2030s, but somehow they still startle us). It's true that, had this conference taken place as planned on 6-8 June, I would have been speaking on the exact centenary of the publication of Nineteen Eighty-Four. But for two reasons I'm actually glad to be speaking in October.

The first is that today marks a different centenary: that of the founding of the People's Republic of China. This is significant as my specialty in Orwell Studies has long been the author's relevance for understanding the PRC. My first publication in the field, for example, was a 2003 essay, China's Brave New World, which argued that, though the PRC is often described as "Orwellian", it is useful to think of it as a place where rulers borrow tricks from the playbooks of Aldous Huxley's →

1949

→ most famous novel as well as his former Eton student George Orwell's.

The second reason I am glad to be addressing you in October 2049 is that a key document in the never-ending Orwell-Huxley debate was written in October 1949. I mean, of course, the letter that Huxley wrote to his former pupil after reading Nineteen Eighty-Four. Huxley told Orwell that the novel was wonderful, as the critics said, but that he felt it erred in portraying autocrats of the future as relying on "boot-on-the-face" techniques. Surely, they would find "less arduous ways" of keeping the populace in line – distracting them and manipulating their desires, as the rulers did in Brave New World.

I have learned so much during this conference that I could devote all of my remarks to its highlights. I was fascinated, for example, by Ursula Bradbury's argument that to understand the politics of the moon since the age of lunar imperialism began with China and Israel establishing colonies there in 2028, we should forget Orwell and Huxley and focus instead on The Clone Who Spoke in Riddles, the 2034 masterpiece by Montreal-based novelist Koon-Chung Mandel.

And wasn't Ursula Bradbury's opening keynote on The Canadian Turn in Dystopian Fiction marvellous? It was hardly novel for her to claim that The Clone Who Spoke in Riddles is the 21st century futuristic novel that has come closest to matching Nineteen Eighty-Four's influence, but I hadn't realised until listening to Bradbury that Mandel's masterpiece was published exactly half-a-century after a key year in the history of Canadian letters. 1984. In that year, as Bradbury notes, 2023 Nobel laureate Margaret Atwood was working away at →

→ the first installment of her Handmaid trilogy and fellow Canadian William Gibson published his cyberpunk classic Neuromancer, which some wags describe as The Clone minus the climate collapse scenes.

Rather than say more about other presentations, though, I want to ask that you indulge an old man (I turn 89 in January) by allowing me to describe a play I once dreamed of writing. I thought of it as an homage of sorts to 2022 Nobel Laureate Tom Stoppard's Travesties, which imagined what might have happened if Lenin and James Joyce crossed paths with Dadaist poet Tristan Tsara when all three were living in Zurich in 1917. My work, which I planned to call The Huxley Papers, would begin with an exchange at Eton, in that same year of the first Russian Revolution, between the future author of Brave New World and a teenage Eric Blair.

After that scene, the play would become a one-man show. Alone on stage would be Huxley reading out his 1949 letter to Orwell, and then, as a ghost, reading out letters written in other years ending in nine. The conceit would be that after death we are able to follow the news about one country and correspond once a decade with one deceased person. Huxley would follow news about China and write to Orwell.

In his 1989 epistle, he would lament seeing "boot-on-the-face" tactics end peaceful protests in Beijing. In his 1999 one, however, he would argue that rising consumerism in the PRC brought Brave New World to mind. In his 2019 letter, he would write about indoctrination camps in Xinjiang fitting with dark visions of Big Brother control, but note that the bread-and-circuses side of Shanghai, with its mega-malls and streaming videos that induce smiles as predictably as soma, fit in with his own portrayal of the future.

I never wrote that play. As Henry James noted in a "preface" to The Aspern Papers, while the "historian" longs for "more documents than he can really use", the "dramatist" longs for "more liberties than he can really take". I never felt right trading my historian's hat for a dramatist's chapeau.

Had I learned to take liberties and completed my Stoppard-like play, however, I would now have to write a final scene dealing with 2049. I would have Huxley write a letter reflecting on the recent meme-driven mass movement that some are calling "Tiananmen 2.0" - a struggle that, thankfully, ended without a repeat of 1989's massacres and with the Chinese Communist Party still in control but finally pushed definitively onto a liberalising course.

Having come to the end of my allotted time, I can't say more about that letter. As you mingle at the conference-closing party, though, please compare notes on the words Huxley might use to describe how Brave New World, Nineteen Eighty-Four or both can help us think about the newest shifts in the protean PRC.

....

Jeffrey Wasserstrom *teaches history at the University of California, Irvine. He is the co-author of the third edition of China in the 21st Century: What Everyone Needs to Know and author of China's Brave New World - And Other Tales for Global Times*

See.
Touch.
Smell.
Hear.
Buy.

Over 300 magazines in stock now.

MAGCULTURE
270 St John Street
Clerkenwell
London EC1V 4PE

Online too,
for worldwide shipping:
magculture.com/shop

Protesting through poetry

Romanian poet **Radu Vancu** speaks to **Lewis Jennings** about the power of words and silence

48(01): 100/105 | DOI: 10.1177/0306422019840159

LEFT: Radu Vancu with a demonstrator holding up lines of poetry in Sibiu, Romania

WHEN IT COMES to voicing dissent in his hometown of Sibiu, in Transylvania, Romania, Radu Vancu employs what he considers to be the most effective weapon in making noise: silence.

"Every day at noon, we come in front of the headquarters of the Social Democratic Party (PSD) and we silently stare at their windows in order to show them that we see them, that we know they cannot hide from us, that we know that they are trying to annihilate the rule of law in Romania," he said.

"We use silence because they cannot manipulate it. With marching and chanting they say we are violent, that we are hooligans, that we are trying to violently overthrow a democratic regime."

A daily occurrence since 11 December 2017, his protests regularly attract crowds of 50 to 100 people, bringing together all walks of life – from engineers to students to artists. More than 45,000 people took part in a rally on 5 February 2017 – an astonishing figure that is nearly one third of Sibiu's population.

When we spoke, Vancu had just returned from protesting against a law that, if passed, would grant amnesty to officials sentenced for corruption.

The poet has become a leading figure in protests against the government of a country he believes is blighted by deep political conflict – something that he highlights in his poems which are part of his Superpowers series, translated into English for the first time below.

Romanian Prime Minister Viorica Dăncilă has spoken twice in the European Parliament about the proposed law that would decriminalise corruption, but Belgian former prime minister and Liberal MEP Guy Verhofstadt, opposes it and has threatened to trigger Article 7 of the Treaty on European Union over the issue.

Tensions between Bucharest's government and Brussels comes at a crucial time for Romania, which holds the EU presidency until 30 June. Vancu says there are proposals going to the European Parliament about suspending funds to countries which do not uphold the rule of law, and that could be difficult for Romania.

"The civil society here understands that the European institutions can only help us by the use of these sanctions against the Romanian government and, of course, we will all pay for it. But it's the only effective way of stopping what they are doing."

But Vancu remains hopeful for the future of Romania.

"I have seen fellow poets who are very biographical and confessional and intimate and so on," he said. "They are now writing in a more social, direct manner, full of anger, full of ethical revolt. I think it's a good thing as it gives the artists a social function.

"Poets are like antibodies: whenever there is something wrong or infected in the social organism, poems are generated in huge numbers in order to neutralise the infection." ⊗

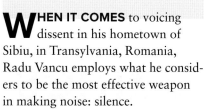

I have seen fellow poets who are very biographical and confessional and intimate and so on. They are now writing in a more social, direct manner, full of anger, full of ethical revolt

Lewis Jennings is the editorial assistant of Index on Censorship

CREDIT: Silvana Armat

Superpowers

8.

Craftsman of children's fingers & the indestructible hair
of the girls & the see-through shields of
the riot police – you've made
a bit of a mess of it.
Today I saw the video clips of the children with cracked heads &
broken fingers, I saw the riot police dragging girls by their shining &
indestructible hair and their shields were as see-through as Your
indestructible light, I saw indestructible teeth smashed in, indestructible bodies
lacerated, I saw the blood You created spurting
into the world You created & there was still so much beauty
in it & that's what turns me to a pulp.
Any quantity of beauty at all turns me to a pulp.
An indestructible beauty in a world smashed to pieces –
verily is Your cynicism divine. I saw a dog
licking the bleeding face of his owner as she lay slumped
under the boots of the riot police, and he was heedless of the kicks
that fractured his ribs too. He wagged his tail with such joy
when she lifted her lacerated hand & stroked him,
there was so much indestructible light around him,
for him evil had passed through the world completely by accident. A
riot policeman with raised visor, a child blond & pure, rushed
up to her & and hit her again.
Craftsman, sometimes I tell myself that You passed by accident
through the history of the world You created, the way we pass
by accident through the poems we write. And that
the hardest see-through riot shields are the ones made
from the indestructible & luminous beauty You left behind. And that
the happiest among us wag our tails, licking the bleeding
faces of our loved ones. Stomped to a pulp beneath the boots
of the seraphim rapid-reaction squads. Terror-
ised by the angels' anti-terrorism squads. Who
could bear so much beauty – and for how long – and
why.

→   Unsparingly gentle craftsman, if it weren't that sometimes I feel
Your rough tongue licking my bleeding brain,
if it weren't that I sometimes see Your shaggy tail swishing
happily – everything would be easier
& more unbearable. Don't be afraid, we're just talking like
the indestructible among themselves.

11.

Craftsman of snowflake and Transylvanian sleet,
when You invented Transylvanian sleet & mountain chill
I'm not sure You were at the height of Your
omnipotence. Try to stand motionless for 20 minutes in them
& You'll see: Your omnipotence can't hold out
in a sleet against which only Your omnipotence
can hold out.
Can God create a boulder so heavy that God
Himself can't lift it? Can God create a sleet so
frozen that God Himself can't hold out against it? Naturally
You can't. Naturally we couldn't. Because You only had
to hold out for Your own sake. Whereas we had to
hold out in Your omnipotent sleet
for our children's sake.
To create a country
that our children
could fall in love with.
(That's something as hard to create
as Your boulder or Your sleet.
But we'll do it.)
The sleet on our Quechua jackets sounded
like kernels of sweetcorn pattering
into a pan. After I left the demo
in front of the PSD offices, Sebastian called. When
I took out my phone & saw his name on the display,
it started to snow. It was if all those frozen kernels
suddenly burst into flower
on seeing his name.
#WecanseeyoufromSibiu, says our banner

→ (it too now alone in the flowering snowfall)
#WecanseeYouaswell, don't You doubt
it. We'll shout until the world
starts vibrating like a phone & then
we'll make the air between us
burst into flower.
Be patient with us:
we'll be the world
You'll be able to fall
in love with again.

12.

"*Bon matin*" (okay, that's barbaric French, but Your world's barbaric too,
so "forget it"), "*Maître*" of syrupy waffles & Piri Piri sauce,
I'm writing to you from Brussels, it's six am, I'm
in a hotel room after a night of rock music & talking about
justice & finetuning Your worlds. "Don't worry," we'll
repair what you didn't get right, we're good at that:
You didn't really get our heart right, we've been repairing it since history began;
You didn't really get our brain right, we've been repairing it since history began.
Anyway, You had to die before our repair shop could get going
more or less, that's how it is, sorry,
we can only work on what the customer brings us. And in this case
You were a bit sloppy with the delivery.

I reckon you must find it amusing to see brains crafting away
inside themselves, hearts with bloody-sleeved surgical gowns
boring deep into themselves. All this blood
has syruped us more deeply & more wrongly
than all the sweet syrup poured over waffles,
and when I saw You biting into Brussels like
a blood-syruped waffle, I don't think it was
just the bad poet in me who was talking. Because
I could swear before any European Parliament
& before any Throne of Judgement that I saw
Your teeth marks in the tarmac. We were singing
Creep, I whispered to You softly that if You want to hum along,

then feel free, but You chose to take a deep bite out of
the night & the syruped asphalt. You know very well
why.

Six people talking about justice in the frozen rain. Hours
and hours. Months & years on end. If I were You, I'd tattoo it
on the hand with which You created us. Or, if You have enough room
on Your forearm (and I know You have), You could tattoo the 600,000
phones raised in Your direction, demanding justice. You'd have
a forearm cooler
than all the eye-studded wings of the cherubim put
together. And You really deserve it. Six people
or 600,000. And the same heart syruping
everybody in its shining & too sweet blood.
Or You could tattoo us on Your forearm in Your shining
& too sweet blood. If I were You,
I'd say it was worth all the toil. (And I really
will be You, isn't that what You once said, and if
we won't be You, we'll stand & and we'll look at You
in silence, for years & centuries on end, in the frozen
rain.)

I look at the picture of Sebastian on my phone &
go to bed. And I know that the blood that
flows through my heart when I look at the picture is
his blood & Your blood. It would be better
if You left it that way. Otherwise, as I said,
I'll look at You in silence until You
repair it. And if You don't repair it,
then we will repair it. On earth
as it is in hearts.

....

*Translated by **Alistair Ian Blyth***

***Radu Vancu** is an award-winning Romanian poet. He works as an associate professor at the Lucian Blaga University in Sibiu. He is also editor-in-chief of Revista Transilvania - as well as an editor at the Poesis International magazine*

INDEX AROUND THE WORLD

Shooting the messengers

Threats to press freedom in Europe are rife.
Lewis Jennings reviews Index's latest work

48(01): 106/108 I DOI: 10.1177/0306422019840161

"**IT'S VERY WORRYING** from a freedom of expression perspective," Joy Hyvarinen, head of advocacy at Index, said about the UK's controversial Counter-Terrorism and Border Security Bill. "It brings in changes that will make things more difficult for journalists and it impacts our press freedom."

The law, which proposes "several threats" to press freedom, was amended by the government after Index, along with other leading human rights groups, urged members of parliament to consider its impact on freedom of expression.

Of special concern to Hyvarinen are the new special security measures, which give police powers to stop, search and detain at borders.

"Those powers are very intrusive, and the protection for journalists and confidential sources are very inadequate," she said.

"One positive thing is that the government has committed to an independent review of the Prevent programme, which is supposed to help vulnerable people who are at risk of radicalisation."

This programme introduced legal requirements for institutions such as the National Health Service, schools and councils to report suspected terrorists. However, it has come under criticism for targeting Muslims.

Challenges to press freedom are not restricted to the UK. Index has been tracking press violations across Europe over the last four and a half years as part of its Mapping Media Freedom project. This quarter MMF published three new reports detailing numerous attacks on journalists in EU member states.

Assistant editor Paula Kennedy said: "In France, journalists covering *gilets jaunes* anti-government protests have been verbally abused, and in several cases physically assaulted, by demonstrators suspicious that the mainstream media are not sufficiently sympathetic to their cause.

"In Serbia, a government-backed news weekly mounted a sustained campaign of abuse directed at independent and critical journalists and media outlets, calling them 'traitors and collaborators with the enemies of Serbia'.

"And in Poland, the public broadcaster TVP continued to present the news in a way designed to show the government in the most favourable light possible and to depict opponents of the government as lacking in patriotism."

Kennedy warned that it was not only in eastern Europe where threats to media freedom were prevalent, emphasising how incursions in Malta were further undermining press freedom.

"The investigative journalism outlet The Shift recently came under a sustained cyber-attack after it published a series of revelations about apparently dubious deals concluded by the Maltese government with healthcare providers," she said.

Sean Gallagher, head of content at Index, recently spoke to students from Cardiff and Fordham universities about media freedom. He believes it is vital for students to know about what Index does.

He said: "It's important for students to understand the implications of freedom of speech in an academic environment and how, through freedom of speech, the ideas and materials that they are evaluating throughout their education can be critiqued and learned from.

"A lot of what is happening on campus is actually academic freedom. It's debating, people stating their point of view. I don't see that being in and of itself a crisis.

"I think the way it is interpreted by segments of the press - manipulated, blown up and used to bludgeon students who are on one end of the political spectrum versus the other, and to dismiss

RIGHT: The new youth advisory board. From left to right (clockwise): Gunyeop Lee, South Korea; Melat Eskender, USA; Emma Quaedvlieg, Serbia; Arpitha Desai, India; Melissa Zisengwe, Zimbabwe; Kate Nicholson, UK; Anh Nguyen, Vietnam; and Oliver Jones, UK

them as snowflakes or to say that they stifle free speech - that is the problem."

Helen Galliano, head of strategic events and partnerships at Index, believes freedom is a subject not discussed enough.

She ran a day-long programme called Unspeakable, which focused on censorship, at the Essex Book Festival for its 20th anniversary in March 2019 at the University of Essex.

She said: "It's opening up the conversation and debate, and this is very much bringing it to students' doorsteps to get them involved in important conversations."

In the past quarter, the Index team spoke on panels around the world and Index held its own events, too. The magazine launch took the form of a debate at Foyles bookshop, in London. The topic was taboos surrounding birth, marriage and death. More than 100 people came to the event and the speakers, including Irish author Emilie Pine and Chinese novelist Xinran, talked about things that women around the world have often found impossible to discuss – from stillborn children in Ireland to the one-child policy in China.

Index is also debating freedom of expression issues with young people around the world through its youth advisory board, which recently appointed nine representatives aged between 16 and 25. They meet monthly online.

Members come from countries including India, Serbia, South Korea and the USA. Topics addressed so far include the future of community journalism and limitations to media freedom.

One member, Melissa Zisengwe, a Zimbabwean journalist, talked about constraints on the media in South Africa. She said: "The minister of communications prevented some journalists from covering protests that were happening outside an event held by the political party in charge of South Africa right now.

"In a democracy, no minister should be able to prevent journalists from doing their jobs because

there is no democracy without a free media [or] where journalists cannot do their jobs."

Index's Freedom of Expression Awards will take place at a ceremony held in The May Fair Hotel, London, on 4 April 2019.

The awards, which are entering their 19th year, celebrate the extraordinary courage and creativity of some of the world's greatest →

In France, journalists covering gilets jaunes anti-government protests have been verbally abused, and in several cases physically assaulted

A lot of what is happening on campus is actually academic freedom. It's debating - people stating their point of view. I don't see that being in and of itself a crisis

RIGHT: Head of advocacy Joy Hyvarinen attends the Cartooning Global Forum 2018

→ journalists, artists, campaigners and digital activists.

This year, Index received more than 250 nominations, with 15 making the final shortlist in arts, campaigning, digital activism and journalism categories.

Nominees include El Madina, a group of Egyptian artists combining art and protest; Media Rights Agenda who campaign for media freedom in Nigeria; Zehra Dogan, a Kurdish painter who produced art behind bars (she has now been released); Ms. Saffaa whose murals highlight women's rights and human rights violations in Saudi Arabia; and Cameroonian journalist Mimi Mefo. The judges this year are award-winning investigative journalist Maria Ressa, actor Khalid Abdalla, social activist Nimco Ali and computer scientist Kate Devlin.

Perla Hinojosa, fellowships and advocacy officer at Index, said: "They are incredible individuals fighting against censorship and for freedom of expression. I encourage people to read and learn about them.

"Many times, there is a prestige which comes from just being nominated, but it also helps individuals to be just a little bit more

safe because, wherever they are in their countries, people higher up will see that they have international recognition."

Cartoonists Rights Network International is nominated in the arts category. The non-profit organisation monitors and protects the rights and creative freedom of political cartoonists around the globe.

Index caught up with CRNI board member Terry Anderson, a Scottish artist and caricaturist, to talk about the nomination and what this means for the organisation.

"What strikes me right away is the breadth of the list," he said. "There is this insidious threat, this mounting trend towards authoritarian governments of every complexion that will only make life more difficult going forward for cartoonists.

"There's no sign of that abating and, if anything, there are indications that it could get worse, so facing that kind of challenge we need allies."

You can hear the full interview in a special edition of the Index on Censorship podcast covering the awards, which is available to download and stream on iTunes and Sound-Cloud from 11 April 2019. ⊗

BELOW: The panel for the launch of our winter issue, featuring Irish author Emilie Pine; Bloody Good Periods' founder Gabby Edlin; Chinese author Xinran and Index magazine editor Rachael Jolley

Lewis Jennings is Index's editorial assistant

END NOTE

Press freedom: EU blind spot?

Sally Gimson argues more EU action is needed when European countries limit media freedom

48(01): 110/112 | DOI: 10.1177/0306422019840207

DUTCH MEP JUDITH Sargentini is enemy number one in the eyes of the Hungarian government. The Green politician incurred that government's anger when she persuaded the European Parliament to the country losing voting rights.

She accused Hungary, among other democratic failings, of not ensuring a free and uncensored press. But since the vote last September, nothing has happened, except that the Hungarian government launched a campaign against her on state television - and she no longer feels safe to travel there.

"[The government] has been spreading so much hate against me, and if the government is spreading hate, what if there is a lunatic around? I'm not taking the risk," she said.

"The Hungarian government spent 18 million euros on a publicity campaign against me, after I won the vote - with TV commercials and a full-page advertisement with my face on it." The other vocal critic of Hungary, Belgian Liberal MEP and former Belgian prime minister Guy Verhofstadt, as well as the philanthropist George Soros were targeted in the same campaign.

With the European elections coming up in May 2019, and the possibility of large gains by nationalist, populist parties, the question is what the EU can do to curb freedom of expression violations on its territory.

The problem according to Lutz Kinkel, managing director of the European Centre for Press and Media Reform, is the EU has no

specific competences over media freedom. No country can join the EU without guaranteeing freedom of expression as a basic human right under Article 49 of the Lisbon Treaty. Article 7 is triggered when there is "a clear risk" of a member state breaching EU values. Although this can lead to a country's voting rights being taken away, to get to that point, all the other EU countries have to agree.

As Camino Mortera-Martinez, a senior research fellow at the think-tank Centre for European Reform in Brussels, said: "Article 7 is never going to work because it is so vague. [All the other] member states are never going to argue to punish another one by suspending voting rights."

Historian Tim Snyder, author of The Road to Unfreedom, a book about how Russia works to spread disinformation within the West, told Index he thought Hungary should have been thrown out of the EU a long time ago. But, with Britain's exit from the EU, it is difficult to start expelling countries now.

"The tricky thing about the European Union, and this goes not just for eastern Europe but everyone, is that there might be rules for how you get in, but once you are in the rules are a lot less clear," he said.

Hungary is the most prominent country in Europe to put restrictions on media freedom. Not only is public service media directly under

RIGHT: MEP Guy Verhofstadt launches a billboard campaign against the policies of Hungary's Prime Minister Orbán, outside the European Parliament in Brussels, Belgium, November 2018.

government control, and critical journalists have been fired, but the government has also made sure that private media has either been driven out of business or taken over by a few oligarchs close to Prime Minister Viktor Orbán. The only independent media are very small operations, publishing almost exclusively on the internet.

Snyder told Index: "I think Europeans generally made the mistake of thinking that it doesn't matter if we have one small country which is going the wrong way [and that] Hungary can't possibly affect others. But the truth is – because it is easier to build authoritarianism than democracy – one bad example does ripple outwards and Hungary isn't just Hungary and Orbán isn't just Orbán; they represent a kind of mode of doing things which

other people can look to, and individual leaders can say: 'That's possible'."

This is borne out by Index on Censorship's Mapping Media Freedom project which tracked media freedom in 43 European countries and found patterns that showed countries following Hungary's example including Poland. →

It's like joining a sorority with very strict rules for entering, but when you are there you can misbehave and it is covered up by the group

I think Europeans generally made the mistake of thinking that it doesn't matter if we have one small country which is going the wrong way

→ Anita Kőműves is an investigative journalist in Hungary who works for non-profit investigative outlet Átlátszó.hu which won an Index award for digital activism in 2015. She says not only does Brussels do nothing to challenge Hungary's undermining of the free press but people in the commission are persuaded it is not all that bad.

She said: "Orbán is walking a fine line with Brussels. He knows that he cannot go too far. Whatever happens here, it must be deniable and explainable. Orbán goes to Brussels, or sends one of his henchmen, and he explains everything away. He has bad things written about him every single day in Hungary and nobody is in jail, so everything is fine... everything is not fine. Freedom of speech, the fact that I can write anything I like on the internet and nobody puts me in jail, is not the same as freedom of media when you have a strong media sector which is independent of the government."

The solution for Brussels, she argues, is not Article 7 but for the EU to use European competition law to challenge the monopoly on media ownership the government and government-backed companies have in Hungary.

Kinkel says that this would be a warning to other countries, such as Bulgaria and Romania, which are trying to control the media in similar ways and in the case of Bulgaria giving EU funds only to government-friendly media.

"Governments try to get hold of public service media: this is one step," he said. "And the other step is to throw out investors and media they don't like and to give media outlets to oligarchs who are government-friendly and so on and so on, and to start new campaigns against independent investigative journalists."

In Poland, the European Commission invoked Article 7 because of the government's threats to the independence of the judiciary. The government so far controls only the state media but, as journalist Bartosz Wieliński , head of foreign news at the Gazeta Wyborcza newspaper, points out, the government used that state media to hound the mayor of Gdańsk, Paweł Adamowicz, for months before he was assassinated in January this year.

Wieliński believes it was only after Britain voted to leave the EU that countries realised they would face little sanction if they chipped away at freedom of expression. Although the EU did not collapse as they expected, the initial disarray gave them an opportunity to test European mechanisms and find them wanting.

Maria Dahle is chief executive of the international Human Rights House Foundation. She believes financial sanctions could be the way to stop countries from crossing the line, as Poland and Hungary have.

"When allocating funding, it should be conditional," she said. "If [member states] do violate the rule of law, it has to have consequences ... and the consequences should be around financial support."

But Mortera-Martinez warns if the EU starts punishing countries too much financially, it will encourage anti-EU feeling which could be counter-productive, leading to election wins for populist, nationalist parties. The effect of any populist gains in the May elections concerns Kinkel, also: "What is clear is that when the populist faction grows, they have the right to have their people on certain positions on committees and so on. And this will be a problem... especially for press and media freedom," he said.

Back at the European Parliament, Sargentini is impatient. "It's about political will, and the EU doesn't have it at the moment," she said. "It's like joining a sorority [with] very strict rules for entering, but when you are there you can misbehave and it's covered up by the group." ⊗

Sally Gimson *is the deputy editor of Index on Censorship magazine*

Subscribe

"An archive of past battles won, and a beacon for present and future struggles."

Times Literary Supplement

ANNUAL PRINT SUBSCRIPTION*
£35 / $65

SINGLE PRINT ISSUE**
£7.99 / $10

ANNUAL DIGITAL SUBSCRIPTION
£17.99

SINGLE DIGITAL ISSUE
£5.99

INDEX ON CENSORSHIP IOS APP
A 30-day subscription for £1.49

INDEXONCENSORSHIP.ORG

Index on Censorship is published quarterly in March, June, September and December by SAGE (Los Angeles, London, New Delhi, Singapore, Washington DC and Melbourne).

Annual subscription (2019) including postage: institutional rate (combined print and electronic) £442/US$816; individual rate (print only) £35/US$65. Electronic only and print only subscriptions are available for institutions at a discounted rate. Note VAT is applicable at the appropriate local rate.

For the full range of institutional / individual subscriptions, single issue and back issue purchasing options visit www.indexoncensorship.org/subscribe. To activate your subscription (institutions only) visit http://online.sagepub.com.

SAGE Publications Ltd, 1 Oliver's Yard, 55 City Road, London EC1Y 1SP, UK tel. +44 (0)20 7324 8500, fax +44 (0)20 7324 8600 and in North America, SAGE Publications Inc, PO Box 5096, Thousand Oaks, CA 91359, USA.

SAGE is a member of CrossRef.

Periodicals postage paid at Rahway, NJ. POSTMASTER, send address corrections to Index on Censorship, c/o Mercury Airfreight International Ltd, 365 Blair Road, Avenel, NJ 07001, USA.

SUBMISSION GUIDELINES AND ADVERTISING
If you are interested in submitting a pitch for an article, please contact sally@indexoncensorship.org. We look for timely and original work – either journalistic features, or short stories, play extracts and poetry, with a strong link to our theme of freedom of expression. Please send a short synopsis of your proposal and an author bio.

VOLUME 48 NUMBER 01 | £7.99
ISBN 978-1-5264-99912

9 781526 499912

ISSN 0306-4220 (201904) 48 : 1 ; 1-B

SAGE www.sagepublishing.com
Los Angeles | London | New Delhi | Singapore | Washington DC | Melbourne